In Shakespeare's Playhouse

THE POET'S METHOD

Maurice Percival

IN SHAKESPEARE'S PLAYHOUSE

BY
RONALD WATKINS
AND
JEREMY LEMMON

THE
POET'S METHOD

ROWMAN AND LITTLEFIELD
Totowa, New Jersey

First published in the United States 1974
by Rowman and Littlefield, Totowa, N.J.

© Ronald Watkins and Jeremy Lemmon

ISBN 0-87471-532-6

Printed and bound in Great Britain

FOREWORD

The object of this book, and those which follow it, is to reconsider Shakespeare's plays in the light of the conditions in which he habitually worked, and in which his dramatic art was formed. Such a consideration proves unmistakably that Shakespeare was a master-craftsman in his own chosen, and now largely forgotten, medium. Three hundred and fifty years after the publication of the First Folio it still needs to be shown that the player-playwright knew how to make a play.

The books would not have been written but for the generous encouragement of those who have made it possible for us at once to develop and to test in practical performance the faith in Shakespeare's stagecraft here put forward. For more than thirty years at Harrow School, by the kind permission of the Governors and four successive Head Masters, we have been able to produce the plays of Shakespeare in conditions approximating to those of his own playhouse. Shakespearian playhouses have also been brought into being for us by the Marquess and Marchioness of Aberdeen at Haddo House in Scotland, and by the Drama Department of the University of Colorado at Boulder. We gratefully acknowledge it as our debt to all those many people who have assisted at these productions that we can claim our research to have been not only theoretical but also tried in practice.

Of our many other debts we would both like to acknowledge one in particular: this book itself is the expression of our gratitude to Bunty Watkins for her constant and most practical help in our long task of preparation and her unswerving belief that the end was worth the pursuit.

R.W.
J.L.

Harrow, 1973

CONTENTS

NOTE TO THE READER

In our quotations from Shakespeare we have made as little departure from the lineation and punctuation of the early texts as has seemed compatible with the convenience of a modern reader; spelling, however, has been modernised. We have quoted stage-directions only from the Quartos and First Folio, since these, in most cases, may reasonably be supposed to reflect the practice of performance in Shakespeare's own playhouse; they are printed as they appear in the early texts, in italics, and not modernised in any way (except that we have abandoned the long 's', and the 'i' and 'u' which represent, respectively, 'j' and 'v').

Since no universally standardised system of reference-numbering is yet conveniently available, we have chosen in our citing of Act, Scene and Line numbers to follow the *Oxford Standard Authors* edition of Shakespeare's Works, edited by W. J. Craig.

Superior figures in the text refer to the Notes which are grouped together at the end of the book.

THE PLAYWRIGHT

It is a strange paradox that, whereas of all playwrights Shakespeare is the most generally admired, yet the least admired of his qualities is his skill as a playwright. It is known that he was a poet of unique accomplishment; it is recognised that on almost every topic of human experience he had something memorable to say; it is commonly agreed that as a creator of character-studies, of fine acting roles, he has had no equal; the hardest-bitten of impresarios has a hunch that this fellow, with proper adaptation, will draw money to the box-office. But one fundamental truth we have habitually disregarded—that he knew how to make a play, that he knew better than any of his contemporaries, his predecessors and his successors, how to create and manage the material of poetic drama. He was both player and playwright: his genius as a dramatist, conditioned by the playhouse for which he wrote, and controlled at every step by his personal involvement with his fellow-actors, was not less great than his genius as a poet. And yet, in the process of translating to the stage the texts which we so much admire, we feel at liberty to transpose, to cut, to caricature or to refashion as it pleases us. It is a matter indeed for satisfaction that the performing of Shakespeare's plays has not become ossified in an unchanging tradition: the variations played upon them in the theatre are not only exercises in ingenuity but also expressions of creative vitality; and the response of the plays themselves to eccentric treatment is a sign of their continuing life. Nevertheless from the practice of remodelling familiar material, it is a short and easy step to the assumption that the material itself cannot survive without adaptation: thus we have come to believe that the audiences of our time cannot take their Shakespeare neat; and we treat his plays as if the poet himself was a mere botcher sadly lacking in stagecraft. This is the implication when literary critics have pronounced scenes or roles or whole plays unactable; when actors 'throw away' the poet's words, as if they were a stumbling-block in the path of realistic characterisation; when director, designer and costumier put their heads together to contrive décor and wardrobe and machinery which may divert the eyes and ears of inattentive audiences, and allow them to believe that mere words are tedious. Case-hardened by such an approach to Shakespeare, we playgoers ignore the fact that he had what in today's theatrical jargon is called a 'method' of his own, the Poet's Method, and that he knew very well what he was doing when he provided a prompt-book for the kind of playhouse in which he spent the prime of his life.

The reason for this paradox is not far to seek. The truth is that the plays that Shakespeare made have not been publicly performed since the closing of the playhouses in 1642: because of a fatal break in theatrical tradition it has been possible to judge his skill as a dramaturgist only through distorted representations: however imaginative or ingenious the variations, we have not been able to hear the music of the theme itself. For too long we have subscribed to the heresy that Shakespeare's understanding of stagecraft, of dramatic form, was rude, that his work must be improved upon, adapted, recast in order to make it acceptable to contemporary critical standards.

From time to time a sane voice has, it is true, been raised in defence of Shakespeare as a dramatic craftsman: Coleridge did his best to 'destroy . . . the popular notion that he was a great dramatist by mere instinct, that he grew immortal in his own despite', and attacked those pedants who 'talk of Shakespeare as a sort of beautiful *lusus naturae*, a delightful monster,—wild, indeed, and without taste or judgement'. Pope, although his own critical practice makes it clear that he did not intend his comment as an unalloyed compliment, provided another interesting and significant exception to the prevailing opinion: 'Most of our Author's faults are less to be ascribed to his wrong judgement as a Poet, than to his right judgement as a Player.' Nevertheless the currency of the critical idea that Shakespeare was an intuitive genius with an untrustworthy theatrical judgement has been astonishingly persistent. It is not surprising that Voltaire, nurtured in the tradition of the classical unities, should have described him thus: 'Il avait un génie plein de force et de fécondité, de naturel et de sublime, sans la moindre étincelle de bon goût et sans la moindre connaissance des règles.' But even Doctor Johnson, whose opinions were a healthy counterblast to what Coleridge later called 'the vulgar abuse of Voltaire', could describe Shakespeare's plots as 'often so loosely formed, that a very slight consideration may improve them, and so carelessly pursued, that he seems not always fully to comprehend his own design'. In ANTONY AND CLEOPATRA, for instance, 'the events, of which the principal are described according to history, are produced without any art of connexion or care of disposition'. This kind of reservation has often gone hand in hand with a genuine reverence for Shakespeare: in the Prologue to his version of THE TEMPEST Dryden wrote (apparently without irony):

> So from old Shakespeare's honour'd dust, this day
> Springs up and buds a new reviving play.

And every student of Shakespeare is familiar with Lamb's uncompromising judgement on the central role in a play that he much admired: 'The Lear of Shakespeare cannot be acted.'

Above all, the history of Shakespeare's plays in performance, from the Restoration of 1660 up to our own day, indicates that the men of the theatre themselves have not cared fully to place their trust in the playwright's skill. Perhaps the general position is best summed up by the particular attitude of Nahum Tate towards KING LEAR: he called it 'a Heap of Jewels, unstrung and unpolisht', and when he perverted the play for performance, he certainly believed that he was endowing it with the virtues of 'Regularity and Probability'. Tate's criticism, it will be noticed, is different from Pope's; not that Shakespeare was undiscriminating as a poet, but that his ideas, however remarkable, had not been moulded for the stage into a workable and effective form; that he did not know how to make a play.

The heresy still persists. Even before the closing of the theatres in 1642 the tradition of the poetic drama in which Shakespeare worked had come under fire, and with the reopening of the theatres at the Restoration a fundamentally different method of stagecraft established itself, and the theatrical tradition which evolved from it has continued with little change until today. Where Shakespeare's plays have not responded to an alien tradition, they have generally been considered to be ill made; as a result, most directors have proceeded on the assumption that they must be remade or modified to suit the new conditions. The proper antidote to the poison of this belief is to reconstruct (as far as possible) the conditions for which they were written, and examine them in this light: and until this is systematically and comprehensively done, the quality of Shakespeare's dramatic range and skills cannot be fully assessed. C. Walter Hodges makes the point clear when he writes (*The Globe Restored*, 1968 edition, 9) that 'the presentations of the Elizabethan theatre were expressed in an artistic style which was different from ours, and which was largely abandoned in favour of the scenery theatre, not because it was essentially inferior to it, but because at a time of transition the scenery theatre had all the glamour of aristocratic taste and of magic novelty to back it up'. Hodges, observing that 'the question of comparative quality is not the point', rightly dismisses the suggestion that one theatrical tradition was, in itself and for its own purposes, better or worse than the other. 'The Elizabethan style, however,' he continues, 'still remains to be explored and developed from where it left off, and contains, fully ripened and ready for planting, the seeds of a different kind of theatrical experience from the one we are accustomed to.'

This fundamental difference can be simply stated. The Elizabethan playhouse depended for its dramatic illusion upon the creative power of the spoken word. Our theatre of today for the most part does not. The theatre of the Greeks, with its traditional austerity of setting on the hill-side, bred poetic drama of universal theme and cosmic expression: the Elizabethan playhouse likewise bred poetic drama, but its greater intimacy, due to its confinement within a 'Wooden O', could house the particular as well as the universal, the domestic no less than the cosmic: in Shakespeare's hands, it had a flexibility and range far beyond what was possible for the Greeks. What was common to both Greek and Elizabethan, and what is lacking in the theatre of today, was a permanent, familiar setting for the speech and action of the players. Though we cannot now be certain of their form, to the Londoner of 1600 the features of the Stage and Tiring-House were so familiar that they could be ignored at the will of the dramatist, or used by him for the setting of some episode in his drama. It was the spoken word that controlled what Shakespeare's audience saw: the words contained and created the drama.

We propose, then, to turn our backs on the universal practice, which begins with the assumption that the plays need remaking, and to examine the possibility that they are, on the contrary, very well made. They were designed as poetic drama; that is, drama in which language is the chief instrument for the creation of dramatic illusion. More than three centuries of alien theatrical practice have obscured this fundamental truth. In Shakespeare's playhouse it appeared unclouded. A reconstruction (as near as it can be made) of Shakespeare's plays in the conditions of his playhouse would, we believe, bring a clearer understanding of the nature of Shakespeare's dramatic craftsmanship.

Any demand for a practical reconstruction of this kind in the theatre will be countered by at least three objections: first, that we are taking away Shakespeare's 'universality' and turning him into a museum-writer, of one age but not for all time: second, that as there have been technical improvements in the theatre since his day, it is obtuse and wasteful not to use them; they could only improve the presentation of his plays, and Shakespeare himself would have relished them: third, that we are limiting the function of the director, who should have the privilege of interpreting the work of a dead dramatist as he pleases.

First, we need to clear our heads about the meaning of this word 'universal'. There is a naïvely arrogant parochialism about the supposition that the realities of our own time are, by the mere fact of their being contemporary, to be considered 'universal', whereas the experiences of past ages, because they happened before we were born, are out-of-date, old-fashioned, bound up with the particular oddities of their period, and therefore need to be translated into the idiom of contemporary thought before they can appeal to the sophisticated taste of a modern audience. Such translation is seldom, if ever, comprehensive. It is easy enough to discover in Shakespeare's plays elements which by coincidence find an echo in our own world. But the director who stresses these coincidences by, for instance, dressing the Roman patricians of CORIOLANUS in the uniforms of Nazi Germany, or converting THE TEMPEST into a parable of colonial oppression, or finding a parallel between Hamlet's predicament and that of the student drop-out of today, or detecting in TWELFTH NIGHT overtones of the fashionable preoccupation with Unisex, does so at the risk of distorting the shape of the play, of obscuring and, above all, limiting Shakespeare's complex world, which is concerned less with a particular war, a particular social issue, a particular psychological problem, than with the human condition itself. And if there is truly universality in Shakespeare's plays, it will emerge clearly enough if he is allowed to speak in his own chosen terms.

Our answer to the second charge is that the development in the English theatre has been more than a matter merely of technical improvement: since the closing of the theatres in 1642, the tradition has not merely developed but changed fundamentally and (must we say?) irrevocably. The paraphernalia of the 'scenery theatre' would not have made Shakespeare's task easier; it would have caused him to write different plays. Our purpose is not to speculate about what he would have done with the resources of the modern theatre, however much he might have enjoyed them (and it is questionable how much the greatest maker of the poetic drama would have enjoyed them), but to examine what he did do with the means at his disposal. It will emerge that, so far from being handicapped by the apparent limitation of those means, he was very content with his medium, and constantly transformed necessity into opportunity. The need to create illusion by poetical means bred the finest dramatic poetry of our language: and this truth will best appear if we watch that poetry fulfilling the dramatic functions it was designed to fulfil.

When we turn to consider the third objection, we must recognise that the director's role has certainly come to be seen as creative in its own right. In spite of this creative purpose, many directors will nevertheless claim that their primary objective is to realise the author's intentions, even if this means re-fashioning the play he has made. We are faced again with the assumption that, however remarkable Shakespeare's ideas may be, he did not know how to make his own plays: this process of re-fashioning is no other than Nahum Tate's 'improvement'. There must, of course, always be latitude for inventive interpretation; every director has the privilege to control and adjust the emphasis of his production, just as every actor will want to 'make his part his own': but the responsible director or actor will wish to know exactly the nature and quality of the thing he is handling, to understand Shakespeare's design and the detail of his execution of it, before he proceeds to frame his own rendering of that original. He must in fact know Shakespeare's plays, uncluttered by 'improvements'.

Our proposal, being both radical and reactionary, will be unpopular—with the designers (whose monopoly of the interest of the dramatic critics it threatens); with the lighting experts (who will be asked to do no more than imitate daylight, and when that is fixed, to leave their switchboard untouched); with actresses, who seem (though the threat is more apparent than real) to be in danger of exclusion from the delights of Shakespearian production; with most actors too, because it suggests that they must learn an unfamiliar approach to their art, and seek to master the Poet's Method; unpopular also, as we have hinted, with ambitious directors, because it circumscribes the free exercise of their invention. Let us therefore try to propitiate opposition by limiting our aim. It should be stressed that our imaginary reconstruction is not designed as a 'definitive' production: there remain vast areas of latitude for difference in interpreting Shakespeare's intentions; in the process of making reconstructions, we have not seldom differed from each other in the dramatic interpretation of particular passages; sometimes these differences have indeed been insoluble even by compromise. Other critics (such as Coghill, Beckerman, Bradbrook and Styan) who have viewed Shakespeare's art in the context of his playhouse have differed in interpretation both general and particular from each other, and we from them. Such differences, far from discrediting the method, demonstrate that it is not coldly categorical or restrictive. It is indeed our hope that this approach to the study of Shakespeare will open the way towards a wider field of speculation. Nor do we wish to be understood as declaring that Shakespeare's intended way is the only way to perform Shakespeare. But Shakespeare's way (as far as our experience goes) is the only way that is *not* tried; and this seems wrong; Shakespeare knew very well what he was about.

There is a fourth charge which must be treated seriously only because it is very commonly heard; that the reconstruction method will not work, because the audience is of the twentieth, not the sixteenth century, and we cannot reconstruct Shakespeare's audience. 'The play as it was performed in Shakespeare's own day,' says a leader-writer in *The Times*, is 'now largely irrecoverable and anyway probably disappointing for a modern audience.' Underlying the latter half of this judgement is a strange assumption that the audience of today is somehow less capable than Shakespeare's own of sharing in the experience of the poetic drama. This is certainly a sad under-estimate of our contemporaries. It is true that audiences have changed, particularly in their social attitudes: it would be as impossible as it is undesirable to recapture the Elizabethan audience's view of the persecution of Shylock, the class-intransigence of Coriolanus, and the parental tyranny of old Capulet, or to revive the whole hierarchy of the Elizabethans' 'world picture'. Although the climate of opinion in the 1970s is unquestionably different, our concern is not with this change of climate, but with the theatrical tradition in terms of which the plays of Shakespeare were conceived; and there is no doubt that this can be re-created. This re-creation certainly involves a demand upon the imagination at present unfamiliar: but it is absurd to suggest that the audiences of our time will be incapable of meeting it; they will find the effort infinitely rewarding.

By constant repetition the opinion that Shakespeare's Method is irrecoverable has become an axiom. It is our purpose to challenge this assumption, and to explain and illustrate a process of informed and prudent conjecture by which it is possible, in spite of the paucity of positive external evidence, to guess at what happened in Shakespeare's playhouse. It will be necessary to discuss the circumstances of performance, the architectural features of the playhouse, its dimensions and proportions; the players, their individual identity and their collective practice; the wardrobe, the furniture and properties, the visual aspect of the performance; the music and sound-effects that contribute to the poet's full score; the early printed texts, our main clue to the nature of the prompt-book and therefore of the performance; the poet's 'sources' which so often give us a hint of his conception of the play in performance on the stage. Above all, we shall suggest that the evidence of Shakespeare's Method lies chiefly in the words which he put into the mouth of his actors: it is only when we re-create, in imagination or in reality, the conditions of his original performance that we can understand why he wrote those words as he did; if we allow the words to fulfil the function they were intended to fulfil, the creation of a poetic drama, then much that has been obscure becomes clear, and problem after problem of interpretation melts as breath into the wind.

THE WORLD
OF THE PLAYHOUSE

We are embarking upon a voyage of the imagination. For this we make no apology: any approach to an understanding of Shakespeare's art must begin in the playhouse itself; for this reason, it is necessary to draw in the imagination a picture, however imprecise, of his playhouse, to form some sort of conception of the conditions in which, and for which, he wrote. The evidence upon which such a picture must be based is scanty and confused, and, in the present state of research, positive proof is beyond reach. Prudent conjecture, then, must play some part in our imaginative reconstruction; but we hope (though we can make no claim to proof) that there is some propriety in our guess-work; it is always based upon what we may assume with reasonable certainty to have been possible. Without it we should be left with two fossils—the text of the Quartos and Folio, and the shell of the playhouse—instead of the living organism of Shakespeare's drama in action.

But it is well, before we start to examine the world of Shakespeare's theatre, to draw a distinction between those features which are generally accepted by expert opinion and those about which it is still necessary to entertain conjecture. The accepted features, and a few conclusions which can, we believe, be drawn from them, may be summarised thus:

(1) During most of the period when he was writing his plays Shakespeare was an active member of the most successful players' company in London; until late in his career, he was present at, and presumably taking a personal part in, the preparation of his plays for performance.

(2) The plays were written to be performed by the regular members of the company—the body which was to become best known

first as the Chamberlain's Men, and then as the King's Men. Shakespeare had individual actors in mind when he first conceived each play. T. W. Baldwin is not straining probability, when he writes that 'the play was regularly fitted to the company, not the company to the play' and that 'Shakespeare's plays represent not only his own individual invention but also the collective invention of his company' (*The Organization and Personnel of the Shakespearean Company*, 197, 303). Baldwin assigned the name of an actor to each of the important parts in the plays; these conjectural cast-lists, and especially his theory that 'each actor had a definite line', have been discounted as speculative; nevertheless they deserve detailed study, if only because they keep us in mind of the fact that the members of the Shakespearian company did provide among them the first interpreters of these acting roles which are usually discussed as if they existed in abstract independence.

(3) The plays were presented in repertory—six different plays, by various authors, in a week—repeated at intervals only as long as they were successful in drawing an audience. These conditions preclude the idea of designing and dressing a play as for a long run; the project of putting on a play would not be conceived in terms of a 'production' as we understand the word today.

(4) The company was extremely adaptable in performance; it was accustomed to appear at court or on tour, as well as in its own playhouse. Nevertheless, the plays were for the most part conceived—at least until the taking over of the Blackfriars indoor playhouse in 1608-9—for the public playhouses (the Theatre, the Curtain or the Globe). The physical and atmospheric conditions of performance in the public playhouse, no less than the architecture and proportions of the playhouse itself, were therefore constantly in Shakespeare's mind as he composed his plays.

(5) The playhouse—'this Wooden O'—was octagonal, polygonal or circular, small but capacious, and open to the sky. While we do not know the precise dimensions of, for instance, the Globe, it is safe to assume that its overall diameter was less than 100 feet, possibly as little as 80 feet; and that the diameter of the interior (with which we are chiefly concerned) was considerably less than the

78 feet which is the length of a lawn-tennis court. Yet its capacity was more than 2,000. The performance therefore could touch the extremes of intimacy and public address; Hamlet in soliloquy could whisper to each individual hearer, even in the top gallery; Mark Antony would sway the whole of a crowded audience with his inflammatory oration.

(6) The great **Stage** projected into the audience, which stood or sat on three sides of it. The middle of the front of the Stage was the central point of the whole building. For much of the time it was treated as independent of its background, and it often represented no specific locality. The background to the Stage was formed by the façade of the Tiring-House, behind which the actors attired themselves; in it were set two Doors, one on either side, through which the actors emerged on to the Stage.

(7) The **Tiring-House**, though the details of its architecture are uncertain, was a permanent feature of the playhouse, familiar and accepted by the audience every time they came to the play. It could therefore be ignored altogether or, if such was the dramatist's wish, its features could be used, described and embodied in the action. One has only to look at the elaborate Italianate façade in Hodges's illuminatingly evocative reconstructions (for instance, the coloured pictures in his *Shakespeare's Theatre*) and to imagine a performance of A MIDSUMMER NIGHT'S DREAM against this kind of background, to realise how little the mind's eye of Shakespeare's audience was distracted by the permanent architecture of his playhouse.

(8) Because of the shape and proportions of stage and auditorium, by which an actor could stand at the very central point of the whole playhouse, the audience were not detached spectators of a remote picture but engaged participants, often partisans, on the fringe of a live action taking place in their midst.

(9) This relationship was emphasised by the fact that the performance took place in the neutral daylight of a London afternoon, the audience and the players being in the same light. That light was very much less bright than we are accustomed to see on stage and screen today; elaborate lighting effects and the deliberate directing of light were impossible: atmosphere, therefore, and subtleties of

characterisation and shifting moods were created by other means—
the gestures and miming of the actors, and the spoken word, often
conveying to the mind's eye what the physical eye could not see.
(10) The female parts were played by boy actors, and the illusion
of femininity was created by the same means—the words of the
dramatist and the intonations, gestures and miming of the players
(both those who played the female parts and those who acted with
them and spoke to and about them).

If we are to draw a more precise picture of the playhouse which was
the home of Shakespeare's craft, we must use conjecture to reconstruct
in imagination certain particular physical features, whose existence is
not seriously in doubt, though their shape and position and appearance,
and the uses to which they were put, are still matter for scholarly
dispute. An examination of the plays themselves can help to fill out
the picture, and the acid test in considering this or that passage is the
cardinal question which we shall continually ask ourselves: what,
specifically, did the members of the lively, adaptable and developing
company for which Shakespeare wrote, do with the play they were to
perform and the playhouse they were to perform in?

The two great **Doors** set in the Tiring-House façade were certainly
substantial in height and width, for they served to admit the massed
exits and entrances of a riotous mob, or of an army carrying banners,
pikes—even the 'leavy Screens' of Birnam Wood. For much of the
time they were merely a means of access to the Stage, and the selective
eyes of the audience ignored them when they saw in imagination a
battlefield or a wood. This truth is sharply defined for us in the stage-
directions of the early texts. On the battlefield of Corioli the heroes
are thus deployed: *Enter at one Doore Cominius, with the Romanes: At
another Doore Martius, with his Arme in a Scarfe.* And in the depth of
a wood near Athens, *Enter the King of Fairies at one doore with his traine,
and the Queene at another with hers.* On the other hand, it is sometimes
the dramatist's intention that the Door should be precisely what it is;
and in such cases the action and dialogue will, for the moment, bring
the Door clearly and specifically to the eyes of the audience. In As
You Like It, when Orlando comes puzzled home after his wrestling

match, the Door by which he enters is merely a means of access to the Stage. But in the other Door stands old Adam, and he has urgent warning to give:

> O unhappy youth,
> Come not within these doors: within this roof
> The enemy of all your graces lives
> Your brother . . .
> . . . and this night he means,
> To burn the lodging where you use to lie,
> And you within it . . .
> This is no place, this house is but a butchery;
> Abhor it, fear it, do not enter it.

When they agree to take flight together, the joy of the good old man at being accepted as his master's escort is tempered with sadness, and he turns briefly back to the Door:

> From seventeen years, till now almost fourscore
> Here lived I, but now live here no more.

The Door in the Tiring-House façade here not only does practical duty as the house-door of the wicked Oliver, but also has effective dramatic substance, as the symbol of a life-long happiness at home, to be forfeited at last in enforced exile.

Certain scenes suggest that (in the public playhouse, at least) episodes were played at a window. At one such Romeo, in the orchard below, spies Juliet:

> But soft, what light through yonder window breaks?

That **Windows** were placed above the Doors, and that such a combination (embodied in the poet's words) could represent a house-front, is implied in more than one play. In THE TAMING OF THE SHREW, at the height of the intricate comedy, Petruchio, Vincentio and others approach one of the Doors:

Sir here's the door, this is Lucentio's house,
My Father's bears more toward the Market-place . . .

But Vincentio begs Petruchio to stay and drink, and, as the Folio
direction has it, they *Knock*—at first without success:

They're busy within, you were best knock louder.

And *Pedant lookes out of the window.*

What's he that knocks as he would beat down the gate?

And the cross-purposes begin, comically emphasised by the locked
Door and the intransigent figure at the Window:

—I pray you tell signior Lucentio that his Father is come from
Pisa, and is here at the door to speak with him.
—Thou liest, his Father is come from Padua, and here looking out
at the window.

In the same way, both Door and Window serve their purposes in the
first scene of OTHELLO. Roderigo makes a swift identification for us:

Here is her Father's house, I'll call aloud.

At his 'terrible Summons' Brabantio appears (according to the Quartos)
at a window, and cries angrily 'I have charg'd thee not to haunt about
my doors.' In time he descends to join Roderigo, and emerges through
his own front-door, *in his night gowne*. For the rest of the scene, as the
servants scurry to and fro, with torches and weapons, the house-front,
thus evoked, is the visual focus of the action. Especially interesting to
consider in this context is the careful iterance with which, in THE
MERCHANT OF VENICE, II.v, the poet brings before our mind's eye the
prudently locked door of Shylock's house; how, with unconscious
irony, the Jew bids his daughter

Clamber not you up to the casements then,
Nor thrust your head into the public street
To gaze on Christian fools with varnish'd faces ...

how the Clown underlines the irony of the situation, in his whisper
to Jessica:

Mistress look out at window for all this;
There will come a Christian by,
Will be worth a Jewes eye ...

When, a few minutes later, Jessica leans out at window to greet her
lover among the Maskers below, throws down the casket of her
father's treasure, and finally escapes through the door of her father's
house, the scene is already evoked for us with a vivid particularity.
Well forward on the Stage stood two substantial **Posts**; they had a
structural function, since they supported the canopy which, projecting
over the Stage, sheltered the players when the London skies were unhelpful. For much of the time these Posts, like the Doors and the rest
of the permanent architecture, were invisible to the selective eyes of the
audience, but they too from time to time served the purposes of playwright and players. In the last Act of KING LEAR Edgar leads his blind
father to 'the shadow of this Tree'; Orlando hangs his amorous verses
on a tree; for these trees we may imagine the Stage-Posts served.
Aaron the Moor in TITUS ANDRONICUS is all but hanged on 'this Tree';
the Post, and the ladder and halter for which the dialogue calls, are the
visible tokens of imminent death until the moment when, with 'Bring
down the devil', the bragging Moor is allowed to descend. We may
imagine that, even when the Posts were not playing their part as trees,
pillars or masts, they served a purpose in giving some shape and pattern
to the Stage itself, and some logic to the movement of the players.
The Post behind which the murderers of Banquo lurk, round which
Oswald dodges from the outrageous pursuit of Kent, by which Casca
cowers from storm and portent, needs no particularising identity. The
Posts have an effect of cutting off the forward corners of the Stage
from the rest: the three Witches, their charm wound up, retreat

downstage and wait menacingly outside one Post, while Banquo and Macbeth stagger from the far Door against the weather; the depth and breadth of the Stage, and the fog and filthy air evoked by the poet, create a barrier of distance between the two groups.

The Posts supported the canopy of the **Heavens**, painted—perhaps with signs of the zodiac—to represent the firmament. Although this splendid cover was no doubt as much taken for granted as the rest of the permanent architecture of the playhouse during performance, it is not surprising that it was a fruitful source for the poet's imagery; from time to time we see it anew. Lorenzo's 'patines of bright gold', Belarius's 'covering Heavens' inlaid with stars, Caesar's skies 'painted with unnumb'red sparks', all had a visible actuality. In the funeral pomp which opens I HENRY VI the canopy is denied its brightness:

Hung be the heavens with black, yield day to night . . .

In MACBETH it is a symbol of outraged justice overshadowing the world of which the playhouse itself is a symbol:

Thou seest the Heavens, as troubled with man's Act,
Threatens his bloody Stage.

Like the words 'Act' and 'Stage', the 'Heavens' are part of the comprehensive theatrical metaphor. The canopy plays its part, too, in the metaphor which is Hamlet's image of the world:

. . . this most excellent Canopy the Air, look you, this brave o'erhanging firmament, this Majestical Roof, fretted with golden fire . . .

Important in somewhat the same way for the symbolical part it plays in Shakespeare's imitation of the universe, is the **Trap-Door** in the middle of the Stage, which gave access to 'Hell' below. No doubt this Trap-Door and the space under it were sometimes more clearly related to this world than to the world of the supernatural. In it the Gravedigger of HAMLET sings at his work and turns up Yorick's skull;

with maimed rites Ophelia's coffin is laid in it; Laertes leaps into it. It represents, perhaps, Barnardine's dungeon, where the straw rustles; and the hatchway from which the gentry emerge on to the foundering deck in the first scene of THE TEMPEST, to be met with the urgent cry of the Boatswain, 'I pray you now keep below. . . . Keep your Cabins.' Nevertheless, although Shakespeare seems to have cared little for the sensational irruption of devils with squibs which some of his contemporaries favoured, the Trap was the traditional source from which devils and spirits arose. In MACBETH the Witches' cauldron rises by this route, and from the cauldron ascend in thunder the three paltering Apparitions; and it descends by the same route—'Why sinks that Cauldron?' Through the Trap-Door, we may imagine, the Ghost of old King Hamlet returns to his prison-house, and remains there confined, 'in the cellarage', to cry 'Swear' to his son's oath: *Ghost cries under the Stage*, says the Folio. Antony's sentries, on their midnight vigil, *place themselves in every corner of the Stage*: they are on watch in the sleeping streets, and from beneath their feet they hear the mysterious valediction of the God Hercules: *Musicke of the Hoboyes is under the Stage*.

The Trap-Door, then, fulfilled the practical needs from time to time of the playwright's narrative; the canopy 'of the Heavens served a practical purpose too, in protecting the players from the weather, in circumscribing the acting area, in helping to solve the acoustical problems of a building open to the skies. Yet Trap and Heavens were more than this: we may see them as illustrating the blend of empirical commonsense and imaginative purpose which informed the development of the playhouse. There is a conscious symbolism in this architecture of which Shakespeare himself seems to have been constantly aware:

> I hold the world but as the world Gratiano,
> A stage, where every man must play a part . . .

If all the world is a stage, then conversely this great Stage, lying between the Heavens and Hell, is the world in which man struts and frets his hour. It is a happy tradition which associates with the picture of

Hercules and his cosmic load (the device of the Globe playhouse) the words *Totus mundus agit histrionem*.

Above the Heavens stand the **Huts** from which the trumpet and banner summoned the audience. From here, perhaps, the thunder sounded and peals of ordnance were shot off; properties and furniture may have been stored here; from here too visions of gods and goddesses descended through the Heavens to the place beneath, although it is possible that Shakespeare's Globe did not provide for this exigency. On three sides of the Stage—it was raised to a practicable height—lay the **Yard** where the groundlings stood to watch the play; and round the Yard ran the three **Galleries** where the more affluent spectators sat, always, we must remember, in close contact with the Stage and Tiring-House.

*　　　*　　　*

We have now a generalised picture of the interior of Shakespeare's playhouse; but two important features remain to be discussed. Controversy about the structure and practice of the Elizabethan theatres has centred largely upon the composition of the Tiring-House façade that stood behind the great Stage. From the internal evidence of plays of the period, we may make, as a starting-point, two assumptions:

First, there was opportunity for an episode to be played 'above'. Stage-directions to this effect are not uncommon; there are many scenes of parley from the battlements, like the siege of Angiers in KING JOHN, where the Folio reads *Enter a Citizen upon the Walles*; in HENRY V, an upper level is stormed by *Scaling Ladders at Harflew*; in JULIUS CAESAR, Cassius commands Pindarus to 'get higher on that hill', and a few lines later the slave appears *Above*; King John's young nephew Arthur leaps to his death from *the walles*. We must recognise the possibility (although we prefer another hypothesis) that the Window scenes already described were played in this same acting area aloft.

Secondly, from time to time some sort of 'discovery space' was revealed on the ground level; this may have been done by drawing the curtains of a shallow inset space, or by means of a small boothlike structure (temporary or permanent) built out in front of the façade. Prospero *discovers Ferdinand and Miranda, playing at Chesse*; Romeo breaks open the tomb of the Capulets to discover Juliet apparently dead—and, later in the scene, the Prince's command, 'Seal up the mouth of outrage for a while', perhaps indicates the moment when the space was once again concealed; a direction from the Quarto texts of OTHELLO strongly suggests a discovery—*Enter Duke and Senators, set at a Table, with lights and Attendants*. This area was probably used for purposes other than discovery, notably for concealment—as when Othello, murmuring 'let me the Curtains draw', conceals the body of his murdered wife from Emilia. It may also have served as a third means of entrance to the Stage.

At this point the historian, bound by the canons of his scholarship to avoid speculation, would go no farther—if indeed he had come so far. But our purpose in this brief discussion of the structure of the playhouse is to prepare for an investigation of Shakespeare's craft through an imaginative reconstruction of his plays in performance; and this purpose compels us to form a more precise picture than the evidence warrants. Hodges points out that for an artist to draw a reconstruction 'statements must be made for better or worse', and adds: 'for this reason scholars have been suspicious of reconstructive drawings or models, and rightly, since the only certainty about any of them is that somewhere it is wrong. But the question is one of degree. It may not be *very* wrong, and we ought to be able to create an image of the Globe which will at least be near enough the truth for most useful purposes—that is, until, as may happen, further hard evidence comes to light.' For our useful purpose, too, of investigating the Poet's Method, statements must be made for better or worse; we begin by accepting the existence of these two acting areas, at ground-level and above, and, for convenience of reference, we shall use the names given to them by J. C. Adams in *The Globe Playhouse*—the **Study** on the ground-level, and the **Chamber** on the upper level. It should be observed, however, that there is an implicit danger in the nomenclature: the terms should not suggest that the ground-level discovery-space always indicated 'a study' or the upper level 'a chamber'. When

Adams wrote *The Globe Playhouse*, he was in effect preparing the blueprint of a model which he afterwards made, and which can be seen in the Folger Library at Washington. To make a model, perhaps even more than to draw a reconstruction, statements must be made for better or worse. And Adams's design of a multiple stage with seven acting areas set up a chain of adverse criticism which has unduly obscured the value of his bold attempt to re-create the Globe in material form. Investigations of recent years have made it impossible to accept all of Adams's suggestions, especially those which relate to the uses to which Study and Chamber were put in performance. Yet it is perhaps time now to suggest that the practice of Shakespeare's company in the use of their playhouses was more complex, and less invariable, than has sometimes been thought. By considering the action of particular plays from start to finish, we may find that the use of this or that feature, this or that area of the Stage and Tiring-House, was by no means stereotyped, and that Shakespeare was, in this as in other respects, not the least versatile inventor among his contemporaries.

*   *   *

While it is our expressed intention to go beyond the available evidence, the evidence itself, though teasingly incomplete, is not negligible. An exhaustive review is outside the purpose of this volume, and we do not aspire to make a positive statement in the scholarly controversy; but, before we return to our imagined reconstruction of the play-house, a superficial glance at the nature of this evidence may help to demonstrate the difficulties which lie in the way of dogmatic assertion. It may be broadly categorised under three heads: the scanty graphic evidence in the form of pictures of pre-Restoration playhouse interiors; explicit written evidence, particularly that of the stage-directions in the early printed texts; and the implicit demands of dialogue and action in the plays themselves.

In the first category, the so-called De Witt drawing of the interior of the Swan theatre is by far the most important, since it is the earliest (c. 1596) graphic evidence hitherto discovered. Yet it must be treated with caution. It is often forgotten that what we have is a copy of a drawing made by De Witt, and that De Witt's reason for making the drawing was that the Swan reminded him of a Roman building: 'Cujus quidem formam quod Romani operis umbram videatur exprimere supra adpinxi.' On our two crucial points (of Study and Chamber) the drawing gives tantalisingly inadequate information: first, at ground level, when we want to know what was between the two Doors at either end of the Tiring-House façade, De Witt presents us with a blank wall; secondly, on the upper level, he gives us a row of eight unidentified figures, visible only above the waist, in a gallery stretching the length of the façade.[1] An interesting comparison, presenting us with a conception of the Tiring-House façade wholly different from that suggested by the Swan drawing, is offered by the much later engraving of a playhouse interior used as an illustration in Robert Fludd's *Art of Memory* (1619). It is not known for certain what kind of theatre this represented; it may indeed be imaginary and emblematic. In this drawing there are three stage-doors on ground-level; the central one is a double door which could serve as a discovery-space; above it is a huge overhanging bay with two windows, and on either side of the bay run battlemented galleries; two further doors, a little smaller than those on ground-level, give access from the Tiring-House to these galleries. These two drawings, and other items of graphic evidence, are suggestive in different, sometimes contradictory, ways: we may be certain that the playhouses differed in detail; and it is not unlikely that, just as during Shakespeare's lifetime the drama itself changed and developed greatly, so too did the use made by the players, in performance, of the structural features available to them in their playhouses.[2]

When we come to consider the stage-directions printed in the Quarto and Folio texts of Shakespeare's plays, we find a more fruitful source of suggestion. But here too warnings must be sounded. We cannot always know how precisely these directions reflected playhouse practice: some certainly bring us closer to the playhouse than others; some may come from the author's rough draft before the play was tested in performance; others may be revisions by the author, or some other hand, after the play had been dropped from the repertory. Sometimes the directions are clearly incomplete: in MACBETH, III.iv, we find no exits specifically directed for Banquo's Ghost, although the dialogue of the scene (as well as commonsense) demands that this portentous figure leave the Stage soon after each of his appearances. In the well-known orchard-scene of ROMEO AND JULIET, Romeo spies Juliet at a window; but for this episode (which begins *Enter Romeo alone*) there is no direction, in the Quarto texts or the Folio, specifying that Juliet should enter 'above' or 'at a window', or indeed that she should enter at all. Directions may also be inconsistent, or may vary from one text to another; and they may be misleading to a modern reader—the word *Enter*, for instance (as in *Enter Imogen, in her Bed, and a Lady*) may sometimes represent a discovery. Nevertheless, the stage-directions do provide, for our purposes, a proper and fertile field of enquiry. It is not unreasonable to suppose that, whatever their provenance, they reflected at least what was possible in the playhouse. In particular, we must remember that the editors of the Folio, Heminges and Condell, were Shakespeare's fellow-players; their memories may have been faulty, their sources sometimes confused and untrustworthy; but it is hard to believe that in these stage-directions they would have presented to the reader mere abstractions unrelated to the playhouse in which they worked.[3]

The positive evidence provided by the stage-directions, though slender, is not seldom a stimulus (as we shall in due course see) to imaginative reconstruction. It is matter for regret that the negative evidence has been given unwarrantable weight. In its salutary determination to avoid unfounded conjecture, recent scholarship has seemed sometimes to argue, on the basis of an unspoken assumption (as if the directions were, after all, complete), that because of the very paucity of precise directions, a negative inference can be drawn. This argument itself involves speculation. Much simplified, the reasoning runs something like this: a certain play of Shakespeare's (whatever the implicit needs of its dialogue or action) contains no stage-directions specifying the use of, for instance, the upper level; therefore the play did not imperatively need the upper level; therefore we can be certain that the upper level was not used. The fallacy of this argument can be exposed by *reductio ad absurdum*: are we to suppose that no entrances or exits were made through the Doors except those so specified in the stage-directions of the early texts?

The third category of evidence—the implicit demands of dialogue and action—is the core of our investigation. It is a truth easy to forget, yet one that should constantly be remembered and pondered upon, that almost the whole of Shakespeare's legacy lies in the words which he put into the mouth of his actors. These words are the bulk of the evidence we possess for deducing what happened in his playhouse. By guessing how Burbage spoke this or that line, with what gesture he expounded such and such an image, his posture, his mime, his position on the Stage, his geographical relation to one of the Stage-Posts or this adjacent Door or that distant Window, we may come nearer to reconstructing in imagination the playhouse itself, and—what is more important—the poet's craft in using it. The result of our investigation is not likely to be the discovery of an invariable and standardised system of performance; nor shall we reach certainty about the architectural structure of Shakespeare's playhouse. But it is our hope that an exhaustive and detailed examination of individual plays in continuous performance will bring us a fuller understanding of playhouse, player, playwright and play.

*   *   *

Remembering, then, that the nature of the evidence makes categorical assertion impossible, we can begin to explore the uses to which Chamber and Study may have been put in Shakespeare's playhouse. Perhaps one of the main objections to the idea of an extended use of either Study or Chamber has been their supposed remoteness from the audience. Here it is important that we should remember again the probable dimensions of the Shakespearian playhouse: the distance from the Chamber or Study to the back row of the Galleries cannot have been much more than 60 feet; and, to repeat an accessible comparison, the length of a lawn-tennis court is 78 feet. So the rapport between the Chamber and the 'judicious' in the two-penny Gallery was after all very close. For this reason, if ever the Globe is restored for practical performance, it is vitally important that the dimensions should be right.

It has often been stated, as dogma, that the upper level was never used in Shakespeare's playhouse except in conjunction with the ground-level Stage. Dogma, we have suggested, is out of place in describing the practice of so resourceful and versatile a company of illusionists as the Chamberlain's Men. There is no compelling reason why they should not have performed scenes in isolation on the upper level, if the shape of the playwright's story required such a disposition, and if the actors could command the rapt attention of the audience from that area. That they could do this, there is no doubt; the evidence lies in some of those very scenes which are quoted in support of the negative dogma.

A crucial example can be found in RICHARD II, III.iii, a scene which begins with the entrance (by, we presume, one of the Doors) of Boling-broke and his supporters on the main Stage. The logic of the narrative suggests that Harry Hotspur enters by the opposite Door to meet Bolingbroke; in conversation together they endow the Tiring-House façade with a temporary identity as 'this Castle', and we are soon able to deduce that it represents Flint Castle, where King Richard has taken refuge. Bolingbroke, pointing at the Tiring-House, bids Northumber-land 'Go to the rude Ribs of that ancient Castle' as his envoy to Richard. He gives the order 'March on' to his supporters, and we may imagine that the party moves round the perimeter of the Stage to that area before the Posts where they are most detached from the Castle at the back of the Stage. Meanwhile, we read in the Folio,

Parle without, and answere within: then a Flourish.
Enter on the Walls, Richard, Carlile, Aumerle, Scroop, Salisbury.

And Shakespeare (through the mouth of Bolingbroke) makes much of the splendour of the moment:

See, see, King Richard doth himself appear
As doth the blushing discontented Sun,
From out the fiery Portal of the East . . .

It is even possible that the image of the 'Portal' may be given visible substance by an entrance through which Richard emerges to our sight in the Chamber. After angry parley, the King sends Northumberland

(who is just below the Chamber on the Stage) back with a message
to Bolingbroke (at a distance, apparently out of earshot, on the
perimeter close to the groundlings). There follow more than 40 lines
of intimate speech, subtle in their changing moods, while Richard in
the Chamber plays with his grief and invites the sympathy of Aumerle,
his 'tender-hearted Cousin', unheard—it seems—by the party below.
We are told by Aumerle at what moment Northumberland begins to
return to his position close to the Tiring-House; but the King ignores
his approach, and it is not until 30 lines later that he breaks out of his
self-absorption and calls aloud to the ambassador:

> Most mighty Prince, my Lord Northumberland,
> What says King Bolingbroke?

The gentle intimacy of the prolonged private communing with
Aumerle is remarkable, spoken as it is from the upper level of the
Tiring-House. It seems to support the view that intimate, quiet and
subtle scenes were effective at that range: the compact dimensions of
the playhouse should be kept constantly in mind. We may deduce that
the Chamber could accommodate, without unseemly crowding, at
least five persons, and that descent to the main Stage could be rapid.
When Richard leaves the Chamber, Northumberland returns to
Bolingbroke; and while Burbage is making his way downstairs behind
the Tiring-House façade, Bolingbroke enquires:

> What says his Majesty?

Northumberland answers:

> Sorrow, and grief of heart
> Makes him speak fondly, like a frantic man.

As the King appears on the main Stage, the successful envoy adds with
satisfaction (clearly the King has not descended in sight of the audience):

> Yet he is come.

ROMEO AND JULIET, III.v, presents a peculiarly interesting problem in the use of the upper level; for the early texts offer us two different ways of staging the same long and complex episode. The First Quarto suggests one method, while the version contained in the Second Quarto and the Folio suggests another. Both versions leave us in no doubt that the opening of the scene (more than 40 lines) is played on an upper level: it is an exchange of most secret intimacy between the lovers. The First Quarto seems to tell us that after Romeo's descent, by a ladder of cords, from the window, and his departure by one of the main Stage-Doors to banishment, Juliet also descends (*She goeth downe from the window*), and the rest of the scene with her Father and Mother and the Nurse takes place on ground-level. The other version, that of the Second Quarto and the Folio, contains significant differences in both stage-directions and the dialogue itself: there is a strong suggestion that the entire scene, from the intimate dialogue between the lovers to the violent anger and passion of the end (a matter of some 240 lines), takes place in the Chamber, connected with ground-level only by the descent of Romeo—a moment long forgotten when the scene comes to a close. It is not our purpose here to enter into discussion on the difficult question of the relationship between the early texts:[4] let us assume that they all represent, at the least, what was possible in Elizabethan performance. The implication, especially of the latter version, is that the upper level presented no difficulty to the actors in making powerful and prolonged contact with their audience.

A third example will clinch this impression. For ANTONY AND CLEOPATRA, IV.xv, we face no problem of conflicting versions. Scholars have expended much ingenuity in devising means by which this famous scene of the Monument may have been presented; yet if we may assume the existence, and extended use, of the Chamber, there is little practical difficulty. We do not know where ANTONY AND CLEOPATRA was first performed, but, once again, we may suppose that the public playhouse was the setting of Shakespeare's vision as he wrote. In the preceding scene, Cleopatra's messenger, Diomedes, finds Antony dying from the wound he has inflicted upon himself; he tells Antony that Cleopatra is 'Lock'd in her Monument', and Antony commands him, together with *4. or 5. of the Guard*:

Bear me good Friends where Cleopatra bides . . .

The scene with which we are concerned opens with this direction in the Folio:

Enter Cleopatra, and her Maides aloft, with Charmian & Iras.

We may imagine that Cleopatra, declaring her resolution never to 'go from hence', stands at one side of the Chamber. From the Door on the opposite side of the Stage at ground level enters Diomedes; he begs her

Look out o'th'other side your Monument . . .

She moves to the other side of the Chamber and sees, below, Antony borne in by the guard. There follows one of the strangest episodes in the canon of Shakespeare's plays. In her terror, Cleopatra will not leave the security of her Monument; instead, she commands her Ladies to 'draw him hither'. And *They heave Anthony aloft to Cleopatra*: while Cleopatra jests in her grief, the boy-players above heave Burbage, with ropes, into the Chamber.[5] From this moment to the end of the tragic scene, our attention is wholly directed to the Chamber. No exit is specified for the Guards below—indeed, while Antony is dying, we no longer see them. The poet did not hesitate to use the Chamber on the upper level as the setting for his tragic climax.

*   *   *

We may suppose, then, in spite of the paucity of stage-directions, that the Chamber could be used for subtle, various and extended playing. For the use of the Study, too, there are few positive directions; yet an examination of the needs of the plays is suggestive. We have seen that the Study could be used for the purposes of a conventional 'discovery'; we have seen too that the Senators of OTHELLO may have been revealed there *set at a Table, with lights*. It is likely that, in the last scene of the same play, the sleeping Desdemona was revealed by the drawing of the Study curtains: the stage-directions of the early texts are not positive—two use the ambiguous word *Enter* and the third makes no mention of Desdemona; but all three agree that at the moment of Emilia's entry Othello decides to hide the body of his wife: 'let me the Curtains draw.' It may occasionally have become necessary to make use of 'stage-keepers'—supernumerary actors or stage-hands—for the placing and removal of properties, and for the transition from one episode to another; there is little doubt that such a practice existed in the Elizabethan playhouse, and that properties, even large and unwieldy ones, were often brought out on to the Stage, rather than discovered; but it is not surprising that discovery should be preferable in cases such as these—a lighted table round which councillors are sitting in mid-conversation, a bed on which a girl lies asleep. It is important to remember that, while properties serve chiefly to answer the practical needs of the play's action, they have another purpose too—in giving definition and character to the bare Stage. The table and lights required for the Senators in OTHELLO are properties of just this kind—they are not necessary to the action, but they build most powerfully and economically upon the suggestion already floated of an emergency Council of State called in the middle of the night.

Objections to the use of the Study have sometimes seemed to depend partly on a misconception of its effect: scholars rightly dislike the idea that whole scenes could take place in so confined an area, with, on the same level, an expanse of empty Stage stretching between the action and the audience. Yet this seems sometimes to have been the case: it is in the discovery-space which represents the tomb of the Capulets that Romeo finds Juliet, and the long episode which includes his own death and hers must take place there; similarly, if we accept the use of the Study, the scene of the murder of Desdemona must, to a large extent at least, have taken place within its confines. But more often the effect of opening the curtains of the Study would be to give special character, temporarily, to the whole Stage. They may reveal the breach at Harfleur; or the gates of Corioli which suddenly clap to upon the brave Martius, and shut him in the city alone, and as suddenly open again to reveal him *bleeding, assaulted by the Enemy*; or those doors of Gloucester's house, which are closed to shut out old King Lear, while his cruel daughters take refuge inside from the gathering storm—

'Shut up your doors my Lord, 'tis a wild night . . .'; or it may be the moss-bank described by Oberon a moment before on the bare Stage, so that when it appears, we recognise at once the bank where the wild thyme blows, the bank on which Titania is to lie asleep and forgotten through more than two hundred lines of the play, until that most famous moment when she is woken by Bottom's braying baritone. In all these, and the many similar, cases, the action would not generally be restricted to the area behind the façade-line, but would roam at large over the whole Stage, which would take its colour from the furniture of the enclosure.

Two examples from JULIUS CAESAR will show how the fluid inter-relation of Stage and Study served to give clarity to Shakespeare's swift narrative—may indeed have suggested the form it took. III.i begins with the bare Stage crowded with people; Caesar makes his processional way round the perimeter; Cassius, scenting danger, drives away the petitioning Artemidorus with a brusque rebuff:

> What, urge you your Petitions in the street?
> Come to the Capitol.

While the conspirators whisper urgently, at the front of the deep Stage, of their fear of discovery, Caesar makes his way up the centre of the Stage; as he approaches the Tiring-House, the curtains are drawn to reveal a dais, and senatorial seats. In a few moments Caesar, sitting in the Study, begins in the dictatorial tone of public address:

> Are we all ready? What is now amiss,
> That Caesar and his Senate must redress?

Thus easily and economically does the whole Stage (which was the street) become the Senate-House, the Capitol; and the violent struggle of Caesar's murder (based on the model of Plutarch's lurid narrative) surges all over the great Stage, until Caesar falls at the base of Pompey's statue, beside one of the Stage-Posts. The same play provides another striking example of this interrelation. In IV.ii the armies of Brutus and Cassius have marched on to the bare Stage—that is, banner, drum and trumpet, and officers—one army from each of the two Doors. Cassius blurts out his complaint without ceremony, but Brutus cuts him short:

> Before the eyes of both our Armies here
> (Which should perceive nothing but Love from us)
> Let us not wrangle. Bid them move away:
> Then in my Tent Cassius enlarge your Griefs . . .

Cassius gives the order of withdrawal, and Brutus adds:

> . . . let no man
> Come to our Tent, till we have done our Conference.
> Let Lucius and Titinius guard our door.

Manet Brutus and Cassius, says the Folio. What, at this point where most modern editors have felt the need to mark the opening of a new scene, did Shakespeare's fellows do? The two armies withdraw, by the Stage-Doors; Lucius and Titinius open the Study, and withdraw through it, leaving Brutus and Cassius alone; they are in Brutus's tent. What is discovered? Undoubtedly a table, seats and lighted candle, for the drumhead conference later in the scene, when Brutus says to his officers:

> Now sit we close about this Taper here,
> And call in question our necessities.

No doubt for a few lines at this point in the scene, the four sit close about this taper, and there, in the confines of the Study, the small flame would show to best effect. And, later, at this table Brutus sits with his book, and the taper burns ill, and Caesar's Ghost has stolen upon us. But for most of this scene—and it is the longest, most elaborate and subtlest scene of the play in its interchange of contrasting mood—the action ranges over the whole Stage, which has ceased to be the open ground where the armies met and has become the inside of Brutus's tent.

We need not argue here whether the Study is to be regarded as a shallow inset in the Tiring-House façade, or a projection from it—shallow too, since it must not obscure the sight-lines of an audience on three sides of the Stage. For the purpose of our imaginative reconstruction we need only demand a curtained enclosure of some kind. The likelihood that withdrawal behind curtains was a characteristic symbol to Shakespeare's audiences of the end of an afternoon's play, finds incidental support in the poem attributed to Sir Walter Raleigh, in which our life is compared to the action of a play in the theatre:

> What is our life? A play of passion . . .
> Our mothers' wombs the tiring-houses be
> Where we are dressed for this brief comedy . . .
> Our graves that hide us from the searching sun
> Are like drawn curtains when the play is done.

*   *   *

There is, as we have said, no reason to think that Shakespeare's fellows used the Study and Chamber according to an invariable and standardised system; indeed, our submission is that, given these features, they used them to fulfil, as the occasion arose, the needs both practical and dramatic of each play—and only an exhaustive and detailed analysis of the plays themselves will help us to understand what these needs were. The Study, we suggest, by the nature of its structural position at the same ground-level, was used (except in rare cases) as an adjunct to the main Stage; the Chamber was used sometimes for episodes both subtle and intense, and during its use the main Stage, structurally removed from it, could on occasion be forgotten or ignored. The use both of Study and Chamber contributed greatly to continuity of performance.

More than once in these pages we shall argue that rapid, uninterrupted continuity seems to be an ingrained element in the poet's narrative intention. 'The two hours' traffic of our Stage' might well be an assessment more conventional than realistic of the playing-time of ROMEO AND JULIET, but the phrase certainly implies an undigressive fluency of performance we are unused to in our own time. This unbroken continuity is reflected in the simile used by Shakespeare's Duke of

York to describe King Richard's humiliation as he rides into London
at the heels of the usurping Bolingbroke:

> As in a Theatre, the eyes of men
> After a well grac'd Actor leaves the Stage,
> Are idly bent on him that enters next,
> Thinking his prattle to be tedious . . .

And yet, swiftness of insistent narrative is not the only mark of Shakespeare's art: his narrative is often, also, exceedingly complex; the plays
make heavy demands, in the constantly shifting emphasis of the
action, upon the imagination of the audience. No schoolboy watching
a play of Shakespeare's for the first time (and there was a moment, we
must remember, when each play was new to the entire audience) will
feel inclined to underestimate the problem of clarification. The scholar,
reading by his fireside, may make a leisurely calculation; but Shakespeare, with his fellow-actors on the bare Stage, had the more urgent
task of keeping his audience continuously aware of the progress and
direction of his story. This complex continuity is expressed, far more
often than is usually realised, in scenes closely linked in ironical contrast and otherwise telling juxtaposition. It will readily be seen how
the Study and Chamber, used in the ways we have adumbrated, might
be powerful and economical agents, not only in achieving the difficult
balance of rapidity and complexity in the narrative, but also in conveying to the spectator the strong, sometimes elaborate, structure of
Shakespeare's plays.

In continuous performance, we begin to feel acutely the tragic irony
of the sequence in KING JOHN, IV.ii and iii. The remorseful King hears
from his agent in murder, Hubert, that Prince Arthur is, in spite of
expectation, still alive; he urges Hubert to hurry with the news to
pacify the indignant nobles:

> Doth Arthur live? O haste thee to the Peers,
> Throw this report on their incensed rage . . .

As he leaves the Stage, *Enter Arthur on the walles*; and after a brief soliloquy the young Prince leaps to his death. In MACBETH, III.ii and iii, Macbeth is seen on the upper level poring over the Stage, and invoking the 'seeling Night' to 'Scarf up the tender Eye of pitiful Day':

> Good things of Day begin to droop, and drowse,
> Whiles Night's black Agents to their Preys do rouse.

And immediately night's black agents steal forth upon the Stage below, in the form of the assassins hired to murder Banquo. In CORIOLANUS, I.iii, the matriarch Volumnia teases her daughter-in-law Virgilia with an imagined picture of her son Martius at the wars:

> Methinks, I hear hither your Husband's Drum . . .

The gentle Virgilia cries out in terror 'Oh Jupiter, no blood'; and their garrulous friend Valeria brings her news: 'Your Lord, and Titus Lartius, are set down before their City Corioli. . . .' When the episode closes, instantly the scene already evoked for us in imagination is played out in fact. If the Ladies appeared in the Chamber, the full resources of the ground-level may have been deployed to give effective point to the contrast. On the Stage below, Martius enters by one Door *with Drumme and Colours, with Captaines and Souldiers, as before the City Corialus*; and, by the other Door, *to them a Messenger*. In the centre of the Tiring-House, revealed in the Study, is that ominous gate which in a moment is to close on the heroic Martius. Without the help of both Study and Chamber, we must resort to the stage-keepers for building the wall and gate of Corioli and, at some unspecified moment, for dismantling them. Although they may well have been useful in other cases, it is when we are confronted by this and many other examples of the close and telling juxtaposition of scenes that we feel disinclined to accept the hypothesis that the use of stage-keepers was invariable in Shakespeare's playhouse.

In broader terms, too, we may see how the structure of the plays may reflect the structure of the playhouse. The placing of the early scenes of the sub-plot in KING LEAR on the upper level greatly helps in revealing the pattern of the complex story;[6] the private business of

Gloucester's household is continually contrasted with the public traffic of the main plot; in the third Act too there is contrast between the stormy waste-land invoked on the main Stage and the sheltered interior of Gloucester's house, where Edmund is furthering his treacherous schemes. A similar case can be made out for placing the static, almost oppressive, scenes of Orsino's household in the Chamber, while Olivia's more active and volatile entourage has the broad Stage and the Study for its manoeuvres. Several episodes in MACBETH gain by being set aloft, as if the playwright in the heat of composition had an upper level in mind; and the great fifth Act, so often an anti-climax in the conditions of the modern theatre, seems almost to demand its use: while Malcolm and Macduff and their English allies march and counter-march on the broad Stage below, up above, strongly fortified in great Dunsinane, is Macbeth's distempered cause: the imagery of sickness, and the fact of Lady Macbeth's sickness, reinforce the sense of claustrophobic restriction in the Chamber where Macbeth is cribbed, cabined and confined. The use of the Chamber in all these cases not only helps to make the narrative comprehensible, but also strengthens the dramatic effect of the pattern of interweaving plots; and the effect of catalysis made by Orsino's decision to leave his self-indulgent confinement and visit Olivia himself, or of the blinded Gloucester's unknowing encounter with the son he has rejected, or of Macbeth's desperate final sally from Dunsinane, is doubled in intensity by the descent from one level to the other.

*   *   *

We have come far in conjecture, and it is necessary now to make a brief recapitulation of the features of the playhouse we shall ask the reader to bear in mind as we make our imaginative reconstruction of Shakespeare's plays in performance: they may be seen in the drawing which is our frontispiece: there he will be able to identify the **Stage**, the **Doors**, the **Windows**, the **Study**, the **Chamber**, the **Stage-Posts**, the **Heavens**, and the **Trap-Door** of Hell. But we must conclude this discussion of the playhouse with a note of warning. Our ultimate aim is a closer understanding of Shakespeare's craft: it is easy to over-emphasise the importance of the part played by the minor structural features of the playhouse in the development of Shakespeare's craft. We must never forget that the greater part of the action of each play takes place on the bare Stage, and that comparatively little use is made of the other features we have described. Nor should we forget that flexibility which was a cardinal element in the performing of the plays: often enough Shakespeare's fellows must have found themselves acting in conditions which were very different in structural detail from the public playhouse.

Yet we may isolate three conditions which were immutable, and these are of crucial importance as we seek for a full understanding of Shakespeare's dramatic skills:

(1) A stage or acting area which projected from its background, and on which the action was three-dimensional, like sculpture, not two-dimensional, like painting; so that the audience was closely involved in the action.

(2) A background which was permanent and unchanging, always basically the same (with perhaps different hangings for tragedy, comedy or history, and other adjusted features of furniture or properties to suit the play of the afternoon) and architecturally constant. The audience, entering the playhouse, knew what they would see, and could ignore the features of the background, if the dramatist so wished. The excited interest, at the first performance of each new play, would be—what will they turn it into this time?

(3) A constant and neutral light, embracing players and audience alike, so that the illusion of light and darkness, or weather or atmosphere, or subtle characterisation, must be created by the miming, gesture and posture of the actors, and above all by the words which the playwright gave them to speak.

THE PLAYERS

One of the popular opinions about Shakespeare which needs to be re-examined is the often repeated belief that we know very little about the circumstances of his life. The central fact of his life is so obvious as to be generally overlooked—that for more than twenty years of his prime he was engaged in the everyday occupations of a company of players; not only the afternoon performance of plays, but the morning's preparation, casting, furnishing, costuming, experiment, rehearsal, involved in the process of providing entertainment for six days a week in season, the economic calculation of company finances, the adjustment to the needs of special occasions at court or on tour, the post-mortem discussions of an evening at the Mermaid Tavern. Such activity, over and above the strain and labour of composition, was the whole-time job of an engrossing and exhausting life.

It is to the purpose, therefore, that we should step yet farther into the field of conjecture, and invite our readers to hob-nob with Shakespeare's fellow-actors, to let the names of those happy few, who had the good fortune to be his collaborators, become familiar in the mouth as household words. Proudly, on the page before the Folio's Catalogue, the editors have recorded 'The Names of the Principall Actors in all these Playes'—

William Shakespeare.	Samuel Gilburne.
Richard Burbadge.	Robert Armin.
John Hemmings.	William Ostler.
Augustine Phillips.	Nathan Field.
William Kempt.	John Underwood.
Thomas Poope.	Nicholas Tooley.
George Bryan.	William Ecclestone.

Henry Condell.	Joseph Taylor.
William Slye.	Robert Benfield.
Richard Cowly.	Robert Goughe.
John Lowine.	Richard Robinson.
Samuell Crosse.	John Shancke.
Alexander Cooke.	John Rice.

In all probability the list is not complete. Although more about some of the bearers of these names is known than is commonly supposed, much remains to be discovered; and for the moment we must rely upon informed guesswork as well as upon certain knowledge.[7] For our purpose, of coming as near as we can to understanding Shakespeare's dramatic intentions, they are important, not for the accidental interest of the details of their private lives, but as the daily companions and colleagues of Shakespeare's working hours. These are the people who knew him best. Their total effect upon his work is incalculable, but in our process of reconstruction we hope to guess at some occasions of their influence. Baldwin (303) has a pertinent comment on the importance of such association: 'Doubtless even Shakespeare's plays were the better for the suggestions of these the most expert actors of their age, whose lives had been spent in their profession, although the suggestions may at times have occasioned the dramatist a wry face. In view of the social standing of these men and the training through which they entered their profession, it is now high time that we ceased to brand them as only a source of contamination and pollution to the dramatist, labelling their contributions as only "the ill-conditioned interpolations and alterations of actors and theatrical managers". Since their position rendered them and not the dramatist the dictators of the drama, that drama is their sufficient vindication.'

We may suppose that Shakespeare, whose standing as a shareholder in the company was on a par with all except the controlling Burbage family, and whose value as a box-office draw was unique, did not suffer greatly from the tyranny of dictation. But it is certain that the free range of his inspiration was to some extent subject to the personnel available for performance: or, in another phrase of Baldwin's, 'the play was regularly fitted to the company, not the company to the play' (197). The most obvious example of the influence of player upon playwright is the replacement of Will Kemp by Robert Armin as chief comedian, echoed in the radical difference between Bottom and Dogberry on the one hand, and on the other Touchstone, Feste and Lear's Fool. The casting of roles among the mechanicals in A MIDSUMMER NIGHT'S DREAM may have been a stroke of genius on the poet's part, if we suppose that he invited the ebullient Kemp to caricature himself in the aspiring tragedian Nick Bottom, and placed beside him Thomas Pope, an actor of his own calibre, as the long-suffering but unyielding director Peter Quince. Such a supposition throws light upon Shakespeare's general intention, and helps to clarify in detail the significance of this or that passage of the play's dialogue.

The transient quality of the boy-players' talent—with the voice that might so soon be cracked within the ring—provides its special problems and advantages: a Viola who was intended to sing to Orsino, but must, in the passage of time, yield the opportunity to Feste; a Lady Macbeth whose rare skill had curdled the blood one year, prompting the poet (since the voice next year was still at least contralto) to the subtlest of his female characterisations in the Serpent of old Nile. Especially interesting is the development in the range of the boy-actors' performance: the mainly technical skill of verbal dexterity required of Queen Margaret, or Constance, or Juliet, or Hermia and Helena, advances to the emotional sensibility of Beatrice, Rosalind and Viola, and from them to the ambivalence of Cressida, the alienated distraction of Ophelia and Lady Macbeth, and the infinite variety of mood and feeling in Cleopatra. To trace in imagination the growing experience of those talented apprentices who were first taught to play these parts is to let in new light upon the poet's process of composition. In one of the Folger Library's many copies of the First Folio, Samuel Gilburne appears to have written his autograph against his printed name: he must have been in his thirties when he bought (at great expense, for it cost him £1) or was given his copy, and recollected in tranquillity the emotions of those early days, when (if we follow Baldwin's ascription) he was the first to impersonate Celia and Olivia. Alas, that he made no revealing notes in the margin to perpetuate his experience.

There are sterile as well as fruitful ways of tilling this particular field of conjecture. Something can be gained by ascribing young Hamlet's thirty years to Burbage's maturity in 1601 or Mark Antony's mutinous white hairs which 'reprove the brown for rashness' to his advanced age six years later: but we must not forget the histrionic ability of a great actor whose triumphs included the octogenarian Lear. It is certainly more to the purpose that when he first played Hamlet, he had already collaborated with Shakespeare in the creation of the introspective Brutus. It is perhaps no more than an intriguing coincidence that Heminges, to whom Baldwin ascribes a 'line' of irascible fathers, had himself more than a dozen children. But it is hardly doubtful that one and the same actor played the parts of Capulet, Egeus, and Brabantio; for apart from the similar situations of these fathers of refractory daughters, the verbal tricks of their speech are so much alike that it is open to question which of the two—playwright or player—had more to do with the formation of so highly individual a speech-style. We may add to the list Polonius, whose circuitous iterations have a preliminary sketch in the language of Egeus, and Glendower, who finds the very words of Capulet—'a peevish self-will'd Harlotry'—to express his vexation at his daughter's obstinacy. If we allow imagination to play round the identity of Shakespeare's fellow-actors, light can be thrown on some quite unlikely points of interest: for instance, the Folio's numbering of the members of the mob in the market-place at Caesar's funeral—1.2.3.4. in several variations of order—may seem not at all haphazard, if we suppose (as Baldwin suggests) that one of the Folio editors, Condell, was on the rostrum as Antony, and the other, Heminges, probably in the coffin there as Caesar: their recollection of the vocal timbre of certain key-speeches in the general clamour might give differential identity to this or that leader in the motley crowd. Sometimes one can detect a sort of private theatrical joke, shared of course with the regular aficionados in the audience, as when Heminges-Polonius (who was Heminges-Caesar) tells us: 'I did enact Julius Caesar, I was kill'd i'th' Capitol: Brutus kill'd me.' And Hamlet (Burbage) had been Brutus too, and his outrageous comment, 'It was a brute part of him, to kill so Capital a Calf there', has an overtone of green-room topicality which we cannot share now. Pope-Fluellen, too, has a like jest about Falstaff (who was also Pope): '. . . the fat Knight with the great belly doublet: he was full of jests, and gipes, and knaveries, and mocks, I have forgot his name'.

The ascription of parts (except for one or two documented instances) is of course conjectural, but since the nucleus of the company is so limited in number, the margin of error is not great. We have adopted, with few exceptions, Baldwin's conjectural cast-lists, desiring to be no more dogmatic than he himself seeks to be in the chapter of his book in which he attempts 'to follow Shakespeare's mind in the casting of his characters' (218, *note*). The purist's disapproval of conjecture is a sterile process: and though Baldwin's belief that 'each play was so written as to contain a representative of the line of each principal actor' seems to suggest too rigid a practice for so versatile a crew of entertainers, we can but applaud his decision that, because of the inevitable uncertainty, he would attempt a complete casting of parts. So, in describing Phillips's inflections in a speech of Cassius, or pointing a similarity in Heminges's series of irascible fathers, or tracing the graduation of the tall boy who played Calphurnia to the roles of Rosalind and Viola (let us use the name which Baldwin gives him, Ned Shakespeare), and matching it with the shorter Gilburne's progress from Brutus's Portia to Celia and Olivia, we do not claim to be dealing with facts.

Our principal motive for indulging speculation in this field is to keep the reader constantly in mind of the theatrical ambience in which Shakespeare worked, to remind him that these famous roles were not the abstractions into which subsequent criticism has turned them, nor the neutral material for the superimposed interpretations of directors and actors, but clear-cut portraits created by the poet and his colleagues: Shakespeare knew what he intended, and his fellow-actors shared that primary intention; and if we can deduce what that intention was, by reconstructing in imagination the first collaboration of poet and player, we shall be able to remove some of the over-painting of the 'improvers' and reveal the artist's original brush-work.

Later in the course of our argument, we shall suggest moreover that the task of Shakespeare's actors was not wholly or exclusively concerned with characterisation. If it is not impertinent to believe that

Hamlet, when advising the Players, is speaking with Shakespeare's own voice, we may deduce a little about Shakespeare's views on the theory and practice of his craft. Hamlet, who speaks more than once of the difference between the 'Judicious' in the audience and the groundlings, 'who (for the most part) are capable of nothing, but inexplicable dumb shows, and noise', seems to advocate a kind of dramatic moderation; speeches are not to be mouthed but should be spoken 'trippingly on the Tongue'; a passion should never be torn to tatters; the gagging clown who sacrifices a 'necessary Question of the Play' to unscheduled laughs, is 'Villainous'. Elsewhere Shakespeare (through the mouth of his characters) speaks scornfully of the 'strutting Player' who takes pleasure in the sound of his own footfall:

> whose conceit
> Lies in his Ham-string, and doth think it rich
> To hear the wooden Dialogue and sound
> 'Twixt his stretch'd footing, and the Scaffoldage ...

There seems to be a timeless mistrust of the excesses of undisciplined actors: but it is unlikely that, while Shakespeare continued to write for his company, these can have been the faults of Burbage and (with the possible exception of the clowns) his fellow-players. Perhaps most interesting of all is the point that Hamlet has to make about the actors' mime and gesture. In general, the policy of discriminating moderation continues: 'Nor do not saw the Air too much with your hand thus, but use all gently. . . .' But something more particular too may perhaps be gleaned from the lines:

> Be not too tame neither: but let your own Discretion be your Tutor. Suit the Action to the Word, the Word to the Action, with this special observance: That you o'er-step not the modesty of Nature; for any thing so over-done, is from the purpose of Playing, whose end both at the first and now, was and is, to hold as 'twere the Mirror up to Nature.

There is still dispute about the acting-style of the Elizabethan player;[8] and in all ages it has been difficult to identify precisely the meaning of theatrical naturalism or realism. Certainly, when the acting of Shakespeare's time was attacked by contemporary critics, it was mostly for exaggeration or affectation, but when it was praised, it was on the whole for realism or lifelike characterisation. Nevertheless a detailed study of the plays suggests that repeatedly the actors were asked to go beyond their basic task of interpreting character and narrative. Again and again, they must step out of their characters to serve the needs of the play: Marcellus evoking the wholesome nights of Christmas, Lear creating in word and gesture the storm on the heath, Enobarbus remembering Cleopatra on the river of Cydnus— each seems to forget momentarily his role of common soldier, infirm octogenarian, blunt ironist. These are famous examples; there are many others, less striking or lengthy: the naturalistic actress playing Regan will find it irritating to hold up the swift byplay of her arrival at Gloucester's house for a single atmospheric line—'Thus out of season, threading dark ey'd night'; but it is important to the playwright's purpose, and the training of his boy-players was not confined to the study of a naturalistic style. Hamlet's advice does seem to recognise this pervasively frequent function of the Shakespearian player: the actor who suits 'the Action to the Word' will be doing something more than merely representing character. 'The Word' is the chief instrument of the poetic drama; and within the bounds of his assumed character (so that he does not o'erstep the modesty of nature) the actor must interpret and reinforce with mime and gesture the creative power of the spoken word, illustrating atmosphere, mood, personality and narrative. This mimetic interpretation was not a matter of literal and stylised or merely imitative gesture. It is not surprising that critics of the time condemned a routine of gesticulation based perhaps on the practice of the schools of rhetoric.[9] It will be readily understood that the actor's task in himself creating and sustaining the poet's illusive imagery was altogether subtler.

One thing that emerges most clearly from a detailed study of the plays is that the playwright had strong and positive views about the way in which the Poet's Method should be realised in the performance of his fellow-players. We may be sure that the practical problems were great and many: the doubling of parts taxed the histrionic resources of the minor players; rehearsal time was formidably short; it was unlikely that a single play was performed on two successive days. Yet we need not deduce from these conditions that the players used a crudely emblematic and standardised method—that certain gestures immediately evoked stock responses from the audience, or that stage-grouping followed a simple repetitive pattern. Any actor in repertory today knows how much can be achieved in an astonishingly short time by the members of a company who are accustomed to working with each other and steeped in the traditions of their theatre.[10] It is platitudinous to observe that Shakespeare's plays require various, passionate, sophisticated and profound playing: he would not, we submit, have made such demands if they could never have been fulfilled. Without the understanding co-operation of his players—and indeed without that of their successors today—then the play is marred: it goes not forward, doth it?

COSTUME

We need, if we are to attempt a reconstruction of Shakespeare's plays on Shakespeare's stage, to have some idea of how the players were dressed. Pictorial evidence of stage-practice is slender: there are the three figures (including two boy-players) in De Witt's drawing of the Swan theatre; there is the puzzling scene from TITUS ANDRONICUS attributed to Henry Peacham (1595), in which a mixture of Elizabethan and classical styles is clearly marked; there are three figures on the *Roxana* title-page of 1632, one of them a lady wearing a *rebato* after the manner of Queen Elizabeth.[11] But from these and other forms of pictorial evidence little can be deduced with certainty: our most fruitful source of enquiry is to be found in the plays themselves, rich as they are in suggestion both oblique and explicit.

Remembering that there was no such thing as a continuous run of a single production in Shakespeare's theatre, we may assume that a play would not be costumed, as usually nowadays, by a designer with a unified stylistic purpose. We have it on the evidence of Henslowe, the remarkable business-man who was closely associated with the finances of more than one playhouse, that costumes were from time to time specially ear-marked for particular players or particular parts: we find in his records, for instance, 'Tamberlanes breches of crymson vellvett' and a 'hatte for Robin Hoode'. But there can be little doubt that in most cases the players would have been fitted out from the ever-growing wardrobe of the company. On the other hand, we must not imagine that they appeared as a rule in makeshift or shabby dresses. Foreigners were astonished at the magnificent costumes of English players; and we learn, again from Henslowe, that surprisingly large sums were spent in order to achieve this magnificence. A further source of supply, it is said, was provided by capricious noblemen who, in the constant emulation of changing fashion at court, gave their still splendid clothes to the players. The wardrobe was an important economic asset of any successful company, and it is no wonder that Henslowe thought it desirable to make a meticulous record of the items of dress that were 'Gone and loste'—an inventory of mislaid riches that included an orange-tawny satin doublet 'layd thycke with gowld lace'.

The player Kings and Queens, then, the player nobles and their ladies, must have looked resplendent enough, even in the revealing intimacy of the daylit theatre, while the servants and other minor characters would look very much like their Elizabethan counterparts: the commoners of Julius Caesar, who come in their 'best Apparel' to rejoice in Caesar's triumph, would be scarcely distinguishable from the groundlings watching them. Besides the generalised dramatic propriety which demands a visible distinction between patrician and plebeian, we may be sure that the company wardrobe also made possible identification of a more precise kind: Romans were recognisably different from Egyptians, or from Volscians, English from French, Scots from English. Armorial bearings, if not always accurate, were distinctive: we see indeed from Pericles, II.ii, how they might be used for a clearly symbolic purpose—each of Thaisa's suitors bears a device suggesting 'a pretty moral' from which judicious opinion in the audience may seek to interpret 'the inward man'. Shylock's 'Jewish gaberdine', the blue coats often worn by attendants, Isabella's livery of a nun, the fantastical Spanish mode of Don Armado, the shabby field-preacher's dress of Sir Oliver Martext, must all have offered particular visual identification to the audiences in Shakespeare's playhouse.

There were, too, other suggestive or symbolic uses of costume which are less easy for us to recapture after the wide gap of time which divides us from Shakespeare's world. Particular colours, or combinations of colour, seem sometimes to have been invested with symbolic significance.[12] The god Hymen traditionally wore a saffron-coloured robe; and if we follow Ben Jonson's example and give him a crown of roses and marjoram and 'in his right hand a torch of pine-tree', he will close the proceedings in As You Like It with an appropriate air of customary ritual. The player who spoke a Prologue traditionally wore a long black velvet cloak (perhaps concealing the costume of the role in the story which he would later assume?); on the other hand, with a pleasingly direct symbolism Rumour, who speaks the Prologue of 2 HENRY IV, is *painted full of Tongues*. One item in Henslowe's inventory, 'A robe for to goo invisibell', suggests another recognisable convention; such a robe, combined with the poet's word and the gesture of the players, may have helped the audience to believe that Oberon and Prospero could listen unseen to the words of their substantial fellows. Yet we must beware of postulating a tyranny of rigid conventions: while Henslowe presents us with the bald fact of a 'gostes sewt', we must remember the fair and warlike ghost of old Hamlet, who appears first in full armour, and then, later, 'in his habit, as he lived' (for this last appearance of the Ghost, indeed, the First Quarto specifies *his night gowne*).

It should not surprise us that the poet whose imagery so often suggests a uniquely perceptive eye well understood the dramatic possibilities of costume. Sometimes stage-directions make his purpose clear: when we read *Enter Richard, and Buckingham, in rotten Armour, marvellous ill-favoured*, or *Enter Morochus a tawnie Moore all in white, and three or foure followers accordingly*, we need no gloss to help us appreciate the visual effect. But sometimes careful examination of the dialogue and action of the plays suggests demands not specified in the stage-directions. Rotten armour may have been needed again for the *poore Souldiers* of King Henry V; strongly implied is a visual contrast between the enfeebled but gallant English in their 'War-worn Coats' and the arrogantly splendid French; the herald Mountjoy coolly claims 'You know me by my habit', and the Constable brags of his star-adorned armour. A different kind of contrast is presented in TWELFTH NIGHT. Malvolio affects to be 'a kind of Puritan': his sober black is placed in comic contrast first to his own sensuous vision of himself dressed in a 'branch'd Velvet gown' and playing with 'some rich Jewel', and then to the yellow stockings with which he hopes to beguile Olivia. But the contrast is more pervasive than this: while the languorous richness of Orsino's court must surely have found visible expression in magnificence of apparel, Olivia, we remember, is ostentatiously in mourning for her dead brother; she herself dresses in black (a contemporary spectator was sufficiently struck by her appearance to remember her as a 'Lady widdowe'), and this great lady's household, we may assume, follows suit—the expressive 'thus' of Sir Toby's first line has a visible correlative in his own dress, and in the accoutrements of mourning about him: 'What a plague means my Niece to take the death of her brother thus?' Amid this sober entourage, Malvolio's outrageous legs are the more ridiculous. Conversely, young Hamlet is first brought to our attention by the visual device of his 'nighted colour'; his mourning dress makes a strong contrast, even before he speaks, with the court-splendour he is to mock in ironic metaphor: 'I am too much i'th'Sun.' Later in the same play we learn from the dialogue (rather than from stage-directions) the details of dress by which Hamlet gives visible embodiment to his antic disposition—doublet unbraced, hat cast away, stockings fouled, ungartered and wrinkled about his ankles. It is no wonder that Polonius interprets this disorder as the conventional dress of the hopeless lover: Rosalind too believes this 'careless desolation' to be characteristic of the man in love; but Orlando, though love-sick, and in exile to boot, is, we learn, 'point devise' in his 'accoutrements'. The love-sick Benedick, on the other hand, adopts 'strange disguises', ridiculously extravagant fashions, to impress his lady; and the comic effect of his appearance is pointed by irony, when we remember his earlier mockery of the conventional lover Claudio, who would 'lie ten nights awake carving the fashion of a new doublet'.

Clearly Shakespeare could demand from the company wardrobe not only magnificence, but a range of dresses extensive enough to allow of fine dramatic distinctions. Developing a mistranslated phrase in North's version of Plutarch, the playwright requires that Coriolanus should wear, as a kind of ritual humiliation, *a gowne of Humility* while he solicits the votes of the plebeians; later, in exile, he appears at the house of Aufidius *in meane Apparrell, Disguisd, and muffled*. In both cases we feel an ironical contrast between the patrician pride of Coriolanus and the meanness of his dress: Aufidius, in his own way, identifies the irony: 'Though thy Tackle's torn, Thou show'st a Noble Vessel.' The two costumes were, we may be sure, identifiably different, the one suggesting a symbolic poverty unwillingly adopted, the other the real degradation of indigent exile. The pastoral dress of Florizel and Perdita in THE WINTER'S TALE is different not only from that of the courtiers, but also from that of the true rustics. Perdita wears, as Mistress of the Feast, festival adornments which set her apart from her adoptive family, and which, with her clear-eyed honesty, she seems not to care for—she calls them 'borrowed Flaunts'; and yet in their fineness they reveal her royalty of blood and nature. Florizel, on the other hand, has deliberately disguised himself as 'a poor humble Swain'; and yet his costume is clearly, in its own way, fine too: later, in the course of the comic narrative, it is worn by the clown Autolycus and in it he appears to the simple shepherds as a great courtier; as they acutely say, 'His Garments are rich, but he wears them not handsomely.' When eventually the Bohemian company removes to Sicilia, Florizel and Perdita (Camillo prepares us for the change) appear habited as befits their true station; and as a comic commentary on the restoration of the play's order and harmony, the Shepherds wear dresses of incongruous richness: they have been translated to the nobility and their 'Robes are . . . Gentlemen born'.

With a wardrobe both rich and various to draw upon, the playwright was often able to demand that apparel should proclaim the man; again and again we see that devices of costume may be telling instruments of dramatic effect, comic or serious, ironically suggestive, boldly paradoxical, or emphatically direct in the revelation of character and situation. In THE TEMPEST, for instance, we find many examples of expressive and distinctive costume—Ariel (*an ayrie spirit*) and Caliban (*a salvage and deformed slave*) were both, no doubt, attired to suit their contrasting identities; the dancing Reapers were *properly habited* and wore 'Rye-straw hats'; the courtiers' clothes, by Ariel's magic still fresh and bright after a dip in salt water, were sumptuous enough to warrant Miranda's cry of astonished admiration and Prospero's ironic rejoinder to her 'brave new world'; Ariel's appearance *like a water-Nymph*, the rainbow costume of saffron-winged Iris, Caliban's gaberdine, all play their part in the fulfilment of the poet's dramatic purpose. Above all, we see how Prospero lays aside the mantle which is one of the emblems of his magic, in order to tell Miranda his history and live again his old and human sufferings; remembering this action, we find all the stronger in suggestion the visual device which serves, at the end of the play, to underline the fact of Prospero's abjuring his magic and embracing his own humanity: Ariel (singing of his liberty) ritually divests his master of his magic robe and helps him to become again, in hat and rapier, as he was, the sometime Duke of Milan; and Caliban, scarcely recognising the new man, cries 'How fine my Master is!' In the last moments of ANTONY AND CLEOPATRA there is another such formal ceremony; for her death Cleopatra is invested with robe and crown, the symbols of her royalty; our eyes, as well as our hearts, tell us that the manner of her death is 'fitting for a Princess Descended of so many Royal Kings'.

Most important of all for us to remember, as we seek to imagine the appearance of Shakespeare's company in their own playhouse, is that the whole wardrobe had a contemporary basis or foundation. There is, indeed, what might be called a contemporary substructure in all Shakespeare's plays; he is in this sense the most modern of writers. To his modern conception he would no doubt add a touch or two of period colour where it helped the emphasis of his story: it is not fanciful to feel in JULIUS CAESAR a distinctively Roman tone, but the vision of republican Rome is seen through Elizabethan eyes. Just such a conception of the past appears in the frequent references to the detail of Elizabethan and Jacobean life which editors once fastened on as anachronisms. The action of THE WINTER'S TALE, for instance, is set in an antique past; Hermione's honour is vindicated by the oracle of Apollo, and yet she returns to life as a statue supposedly the work of a sixteenth-century painter, 'a Piece many years in doing, and now newly perform'd, by that rare Italian Master, Julio Romano. . . .' And the gloves, masks, coifs and stomachers peddled by Autolycus are fine knacks for Jacobean ladies. Granville-Barker (*Prefaces to Shakespeare*, First Series, 126 ff.) has an illuminating passage—the more illuminating when we recall the mixed styles of dress evident in the Peacham drawing of TITUS ANDRONICUS—in which he recommends for the costumes of JULIUS CAESAR 'the methods of the Mask and the way of Renaissance painters with classical subjects . . . a mixture, as a rule, of helmet, cuirass, trunk hose, stockings and sandals, like nothing that ever was worn, but very wearable and delightful to look at'. Veronese's painting of *The Family of Darius before Alexander*, which hangs in the National

Gallery in London, is a striking example of this mixture; indeed, when allowance has been made for the fashions of a time rather earlier than Shakespeare's, we might see in Veronese's figures John Edmans's Cleopatra kneeling before the triumphant Octavius of Henry Condell. Shakespeare's text itself seems to suggest that Cleopatra's dress was laced and could be cut to relieve her distress, that Julius Caesar sported a doublet and Brutus had a pocket in his gown, that plebeians wore caps and patrician conspirators hats and cloaks. For the History plays we should not be surprised to find a fertile source of suggestion in the illustrations to Holinshed's Chronicles, pictures which were constantly under Shakespeare's eye and confronted him with an insistently Elizabethan representation of the history of times past. Falstaff fancies himself in a 'short Cloak, and Slops' of satin; and Macbeth, though he may have muffled himself in a plaid, a Scottish cloth of motley, against the wind, would have looked more like a Bothwell or a Darnley than the primitive cave-man of the naturalistic theatre. So in the Histories, in the plays set in a remote or classical or fantastic past, as well as in the Comedies, we must imagine that Burbage and his fellow-players, man and boy, could

> revel it as bravely as the best,
> With silken coats and caps, and golden Rings,
> With Ruffs and Cuffs, and Farthingales, and things.

There is, however, a damaging anachronism in the practice of dressing the plays in the style of subsequent periods; for these are fashions which, by the mere fact that they did not exist till after Shakespeare's death, could not have entered into his conception. When we come to consider the particular demands of each play in the matter of costume, we must not forget to take as a starting-point the dresses of the men and women the poet saw about him every day.

PROPERTIES AND FURNITURE

For the furniture and properties used in the playhouses of Shakespeare's time the pictorial evidence is even less helpful than it is in the matter of costume; we cannot know, for instance, whether the bench which appears in the Swan drawing is a permanent or temporary addition to the bare Stage. Once again, we must rely chiefly on written evidence, and, above all, on a careful consideration of the needs of the plays themselves. We must never forget that for the larger part of the action of most plays, the Tiring-House presents its familiar façade, a conventional background to the performance of the actors, with no specific indication of locality; and whatever the composition of Study and Chamber may have been, we may be sure that there was little room in either for elaborate sets, little or no opportunity for visual illusion or perspective. We do not, of course, suggest that the visible appearance of Shakespeare's plays was neglected, either by the dramatist himself or by those who controlled the properties of the company. Henslowe's inventory 'of all the properties for my Lord Admeralles men'— whether or not it was as complete as it claims to be—proves that the property-store was full of a wide variety of objects of elaborate stage-furnishing. It would be surprising if the playwright who had so sharp an eye for the dramatic possibilities of costume neglected the use of furniture and properties. Nevertheless (although certain items of furniture were specially conceived to meet special demands) the conditions of Shakespeare's playhouse and the nature of the poetic drama that flourished there precluded the possibility of the elaborate, comprehensive or naturalistic settings we are accustomed to today, designed as they usually are with a unified stylistic purpose for a particular production.

The stage-directions, especially in the later plays, are often specific, and helpful in an attempt to imagine the visual scene. But they are by no means complete: the cauldron, for instance, which is the focus of our interest in the scene of the Apparitions in MACBETH is not mentioned in any of the directions; and yet it was certainly present on the Stage, and we can infer from the text the precise moment at which it sank into the Trap-Door. It would be foolish, therefore, to make deductions about the bareness of Shakespeare's Stage from the directions alone. The players interpreted the plays partly by visible enactment, partly by an appeal to the eye of the imagination; but only a reckless scholar would claim that these two methods were distributed according to a certain, invariable and standardised system. We have suggested that Orlando, in the Forest of Arden, hangs his verses upon one of the Stage-Posts; it may be that branches or foliage attached to the Post help to sustain the illusion that it is, for the occasion, a tree; it may be that property-trees stood on the Stage or in the Study; it may be that the words of the poet and the mime of the actors alone served to bring the forest into the playhouse.

Where the stage-directions do specifically demand properties, they are seldom explicit about how they are brought into the action of the play. It is tempting to suppose that while the smaller properties were carried forward on to the Stage, the more unwieldy items of furniture, and those—like trees—by their nature static, were discovered. Unfortunately no such comfortable distinction can be made. Stage-keepers were, as we have seen, sometimes employed for the placing and removal of properties; they seem sometimes to have had a temporary identity in the world of the play: Cornwall, in KING LEAR, decides to humiliate the disguised Kent and calls for the stocks; the Folio direction is explicit—*Stocks brought out*; to the eye of the audience, taking the obvious for granted, they are carried out, not by the company's stage-keepers, but by Cornwall's men or the servants of Gloucester's household, and the swift action of the scene is uninterrupted. Sometimes the nature of the action seems to demand that, before the beginning of a scene, furniture should be carried forward on to the Stage, as, for instance, the table and stools for Macbeth's 'solemn Supper'; it is unlikely that the complicated grouping and movement of so long and dramatically exciting a scene, involving perhaps the

Trap-Door for the apparition of Banquo's ghost, could be confined to the Study in or near the Tiring-House wall. Nevertheless, we must not forget that the Study was not remote from the spectators, and that in its own way it offered a peculiarly telling position to the player: while the front of the Stage made possible a strong and intimate contact with the audience, only at the back, against the centre of the Tiring-House wall, could the player command the whole Stage and playhouse, presenting himself full face to the greater part of the spectators. While, then, Macbeth's banquet-table was brought out, it may well be that Lady Macbeth's great throne, on which she remained aloof from her guests and conspicuously anxious because of her husband's behaviour, stood in the Study, was discovered there, and by its presence lent a special identity to the whole Stage. The unbroken continuity and carefully calculated distribution and juxtaposition of episodes, which, we have argued, were essential qualities of Shakespeare's dramatic art, suggest that the use of stage-keepers was, at the least, not invariable practice in his playhouse. Since the stage-directions are incomplete, and sometimes ambiguous in this matter, it would be unjustifiable to draw a positive conclusion from negative evidence: it is as foolish to suggest that properties were always brought out as it is to claim that they never were. Only a close examination of the practical and dramatic needs of each play will help us to guess what, in a particular instance, the Chamberlain's Men did.

The visible presence of stage-furnishing in Shakespeare's playhouse was usually dictated by the needs of the story's action; and it had 'rather the utility of furniture than the value of scenery' (Granville-Barker, *Prefaces*, Second Series, 136). That most indispensable property, a table, economically transformed the bare Stage into a banqueting-hall or a council chamber; the number of stage-directions explicitly requiring tables is relatively small, but we may be sure they were in constant use: the early texts of HAMLET direct that there should be a table bearing the paraphernalia of the duel in the last scene; it is the action and the dialogue ('the Table's full'), rather than a stage-direction, which demands a table for the ghost-ridden banquet in MACBETH; it is from the dialogue, retrospectively, that we deduce that the third scene of I HENRY IV takes place round a council-table—much later in the play Hotspur remembers (IV.iii.99) that the King 'Rated my Uncle from the Council-Board'. The arbour of MUCH ADO ABOUT NOTHING, in which Benedick conceals himself, the box-tree of TWELFTH NIGHT, behind which Sir Toby and his gang hide, at once supply the needs of the story's action and by their very presence help to transform the bare Stage into a garden; for these essential items of stage-dressing there is no specific direction in the early texts. Similarly the throne on which the usurper Richard the Third is seated 'Thus high', on which it is said that Lady Macbeth 'keeps her State', may be deduced from the text; and it is plain that this important property appeared again in many scenes to lend its particular identity to the Stage, even where neither dialogue nor stage-direction explicitly calls for it.

Properties and furniture, then, were chiefly used for a practical purpose, to supply the immediate needs of the play's action; but we must not ignore another function of stage-furnishing, less obvious but no less important. It was sometimes used not so much for a functional purpose as to invest the bare Stage with a particular identity, to bring a suggestion of locality, or time of day, or season of the year, or atmosphere. We have seen how the structure of the playhouse may have been used to clarify a complex story: properties seem to have been employed for a similar purpose. In MACBETH, Duncan arrives before the castle of Inverness and is welcomed by Lady Macbeth; he leaves the Stage by one of the Doors (as if passing into the Castle), with a playful courtesy: 'By your leave Hostess.' Immediately upon his words, hautboys play, and attendants enter with *Torches* and *Dishes and Service*. There is no recognition of these servants in the dialogue—they pass *over the Stage. Then enter Macbeth*. By a simple visual device the scene has been set for us outside the banqueting-hall; while Macbeth wrestles with his motives, we feel the nearness of the King contentedly at supper; as a result there is a special immediacy in Macbeth's uneasy reminder to himself that he is the King's 'Host', and in the urgent words of Lady Macbeth's entry: 'He has almost supp'd: why have you left the chamber?' In JULIUS CAESAR, I.iii, Cassius tells Casca, 'you and I will yet, ere day, See Brutus at his house . . .' But, for reasons which we need not discuss here, the poet requires that the scene which follows should not be an interior one, and the Folio's stage-direction is clear: *Enter Brutus in his Orchard*. Again and again during the scene we are reminded that we are in the open air, and that it is night, but of an orchard (or, as we should now say, garden) there is no word in the dialogue—except perhaps the oblique suggestion in 'Go to the Gate'. A tree, or some foliage, in the Study gives to the whole Stage the definition of this particular locality, and throughout the scene we feel that we are close to the house from which the boy Lucius and the wakeful Portia emerge—close, also, to the streets of Rome from which Cassius and the conspirators have come to visit Brutus. The garden is a world of its own, mid-way between the vulnerable domestic intimacy of the household and the political dangers outside the gate.

Out of the practical need to set a scene, sometimes, the playwright bred dramatic opportunity. In CORIOLANUS, II.ii, the action takes place, for the first time in the play, inside the Capitol, and the locality is simply established: *Enter two Officers, to lay Cushions, as it were, in the Capitol*. But these officers, unlike the attendants in MACBETH, are not silent: as they go about their business, they speak in racy comment on the play's issues; they are objective observers, neither patrician nor plebeian, and they weigh up the odds of political success for Coriolanus, placing his dilemma in the larger context of their views on social obligation, pride, sycophancy and malice. When, later, Coriolanus returns after gathering the votes of the people, the scene is once more set in the Capitol, and we may be sure that the cushions were again visible—indeed, they become, in a sense, symbols of patrician authority when Coriolanus sarcastically rallies the Senators for flattering the common people: 'Let them have Cushions by you.'

Particularly interesting in its deployment, for the purpose of scene-setting, of a combination of visible properties, the physical structure of the playhouse, and the playwright's words, is a brief episode in ROMEO AND JULIET. The Maskers, on their way to Capulet's house, *march about the Stage, and Servingmen come forth with their napkins*. While Mercutio and his company saunter round the perimeter of the Stage, the illusion of a change of venue is created for us by the discovery, in the Study, of lights, hangings, a table, stools and other paraphernalia of the banquet. That these properties are discovered rather than brought on is strongly suggested by the excited chatter of the Servants: they are not bringing on, but clearing away, the feast: the dancing is about to begin—'Where's Potpan, that he helps not to take away? He shift a Trencher? . . . Away with the Jointstools, remove the Court-cupboard, look to the Plate . . . save me a piece of Marchpane. . . . Be brisk awhile. . . .' When Capulet and his other guests enter to join the Maskers, his words help to sustain the illusion: 'Welcome Gentlemen . . . come Musicians play . . . give room, and foot it Girls, More light you knaves, and turn the Tables up. . . .' We cannot know how many of the properties mentioned in the dialogue were actually present on the Stage (Henslowe includes 'marchepanes', property confectionery of some kind, in his inventory); but we may assume that the excitable words were reinforced by a good deal of visible business. For this transition from the streets of Verona to the house of the Capulets many modern editors feel the need to mark the opening of a new scene; in Shakespeare's playhouse the transition was made more swiftly and economically.

For this same sort of atmospheric or suggestive purpose, the stage-directions and dialogue of the plays demand a host of torches, tapers and lights. By a kind of visual paradox, they tellingly supported the poet's creative word in conjuring up darkness in the daylit playhouse. In MUCH ADO ABOUT NOTHING the gallants visit the monument of the 'dead' Hero, and bring with them *three or foure with Tapers*; at the end of this little scene of elegiac expiation the lights are extinguished, the morning returns, and with it order and harmony are restored:

> Good morrow masters, put your Torches out,
> The wolves have preyed, and look, the gentle day
> Before the wheels of Phoebus, round about
> Dapples the drowsy East with spots of grey . . .

MACBETH, the darkest of the plays, again and again demands the use of lights: torches accompany Duncan's arrival at Inverness and the feast which follows; Fleance twice carries a torch before his father (the second is quenched in the scuffle of Banquo's murder); *a Servant with a Torch* lights Macbeth on the first lap of his journey towards the murder of Duncan; Lady Macbeth walks in her sleep *with a Taper*— it is the light she has 'by her continually' to defeat the darkness she can no longer bear. Othello, according to the First Quarto, brings *a light* into Desdemona's bedchamber—it plays its small part in setting the scene, and suggests to the poet his famous image for the irrevocable extinction of Desdemona's life. A taper burns too (though there is no stage-direction for it) in Imogen's bedchamber: she tells her lady,

> I have read three hours then:
> Mine eyes are weak,
> Fold down the leaf where I have left: to bed.
> Take not away the Taper, leave it burning . . .

And this taper, too, plays its part in the poet's imagery, as Iachimo stealthily observes the sleeping girl:

> the Flame o'th'Taper
> Bows toward her, and would under-peep her lids,
> To see th'enclosed Lights . . .

Imogen's sleepy words remind us of the uneasy night in Brutus's tent; there too is a taper, round which the captains sit; the little light helps to evoke 'the deep of night' in which the ghost of Caesar walks:

> Let me see, let me see; is not the Leaf turn'd down
> Where I left reading? Here it is I think.
> *Enter the Ghost of Caesar.*
> How ill this Taper burns. Ha! Who comes here?

Although Shakespeare's chief instrument for the creating of illusion was always the spoken word, it seems then that he was ready to exploit the immediate suggestive effect of properties and furniture. We have seen that Brutus's orchard may have been created by visible means only; on many other occasions, no doubt, arbours, trees or foliage (leafy branches like those carried by Malcolm's army) served to bring a forest, a garden or a park into the playhouse. Sometimes indeed the poet uses the spoken word to invest the simple and objective reality of these properties with greater beauty or significance. Hero's description of the 'honeysuckles ripened by the sun' is not merely a decorative cadenza; after the broad comedy of the gulling of Benedick, the arbour is being re-styled, with a different, sweeter, more lyrical tone, for the deception of Beatrice. Another useful item of property stock was the moss bank: Henslowe possessed more than one. The travelling players in HAMLET have one in their luggage—they use a Banke of Flowers in their play. We may guess that it made an appearance in the last Act of THE MERCHANT OF VENICE, and was magically enriched by the poet with the moonlight of Belmont: 'How sweet the moon-light sleeps upon this bank, Here will we sit. . . .' Its starring role is in A MIDSUMMER NIGHT'S DREAM: here too it is embellished by the poet, this time in advance of its appearance, through the mouth of Oberon, until it becomes in the mind's eye of the audience a 'flow'ry bed' fit for the Fairy Queen.

Clearly Shakespeare's company could draw upon a comprehensive collection of small and manageable properties, of a kind not always specified in the stage-directions, and not on the whole recorded in Henslowe's inventory: books, letters, scrolls and proclamations; a handkerchief for Desdemona; a map for Lear; banners, colours, pikes and bills for the armies; caskets for Portia; a buck-basket large enough for Falstaff, and a small basket for old Gobbo; coffins for Caesar and Ophelia; a trunk for Iachimo; a mirror for Richard II; a carrying-chair for King John (*John brought in*) and King Lear (*Enter Lear in a chaire carried by Servants*); severed heads and hands; skulls, and generous quantities of blood; pots and pans, skillets and trenchers, flagons, cups and buckets. On the subject of larger and more static properties, those which in their use seem to approach the 'scenery' we are accustomed to today, there is inevitably less agreement among scholars. There is no reason, in spite of Peter Quince's difficulty, to suppose that the Elizabethans were less able to build a property wall than we are. There were certainly *Scaling Ladders* at Harfleur: as we have seen, the Study curtains may have revealed the breached wall too—or the doors of Gloucester's house, or the gates of Corioli. The cave of Belarius in CYMBELINE may have been represented simply by the Study itself; and yet much is made of the fact that the cave has a low entrance—so low that Belarius and the princes must stoop to pass through it; it is, indeed, a symbol of their humility:

> this gate
> Instructs you how t'adore the Heavens; and bows you
> To a morning's holy office.

It is not unreasonable to suppose that in the Study stood a structure representing the low rock mouth of 'this our pinching Cave'. Nevertheless, it should always be remembered that for the most part what the poetic dramatist evokes, the 'settings' that he hopes his audience will see, are pictures for the mind's eye—sometimes amplifying and enriching furniture or properties, but often created with no more precise aid than the bare Stage itself.

THE POET'S EYE

To describe Shakespeare's dramatic craft as 'the Poet's Method' is not, of course, to imply that he conceived his plays for performance by voices alone; nor are they purely literary in conception, poems or novels in dialogue form, coming to full life in the reader's private response to the words of the printed page. The circumstances of his playhouse and the resources of his company were constantly in Shakespeare's mind as he wrote, and it is inevitable that the visual aspect of his plays in performance should be a fundamental element in their design. There are occasions, indeed, when he expressed his dramatic purpose in almost exclusively visual ways. The processional entry of soldiers could suggest to the audience the immediate approach of battle, as in ANTONY AND CLEOPATRA:

> *Canidius Marcheth with his Land Army one way over the stage, and Towrus the Lieutenant of Caesar the other way: After their going in, is heard the noise of a Sea-fight.*

The stage-direction in the Quarto version of KING LEAR has preserved for us the detail of Cordelia's protective gesture which, in the context of the play, gives this simple device poignant dramatic effect: *Enter the powers of France over the stage, Cordelia with her father in her hand.* Later in this volume we shall argue that the murder of Julius Caesar is an episode of protracted and violent action, in spite of the Folio's bald direction, *They stab Caesar.** The turning-point of CORIOLANUS is a single eloquent gesture: *Holds her by the hand silent.* And yet a close examination of the plays will show how even in these instances of visual expression the Poet's Method is at work. It is by skilful preparation through verbal means that the audience is led to understand

* See *page* 107, *below.*

the full dramatic import of the movement of armies in ANTONY AND CLEOPATRA. After the event, and again by verbal means, our interpretation of the physical circumstances of Caesar's death is more than once directed by the poet. The expressive power of Coriolanus's gesture of defeat and reconciliation is the greater because it is a carefully calculated climax: it comes hard upon the fifty-odd impassioned lines of Volumnia's great speech of appeal; during them our attention has specifically been focused on his silence—'Speak to me Son. . . . Why dost not speak? . . . here he lets me prate Like one i'th'Stocks. . . . He turns away. . . .' And the crescendo of Volumnia's speech ends in bitter mockery of her own eloquence:

> . . . yet give us our dispatch:
> I am hush'd until our City be afire,
> And then I'll speak a little.

The mute gesture which follows this tirade is testimony not only to the playwright's acute eye, but also to the poet's attentive ear, which tells him how silence itself may be made expressive.

Shakespeare's habitual practice was to demand from his audience a responsive collaboration between the physical eye and the eye of the imagination: he did not hesitate to use the visual resources available to him (the features of the playhouse, items of costume, stage-property and furniture, the action, posture, gesture, appearance, grouping and movement of the players); but it was by the Poet's Method, by the spoken word, that he invested these things with dramatic reality, enriched them with special significance, clarified the spectator's understanding or coloured his interpretation of them, integrated them into the complex unity of the play. We cannot reduce his method to a regular formula. In order to represent a hill, for instance, he used in JULIUS CAESAR the shape of the playhouse, with direct symbolic effect. Cassius commands Pindarus to 'get higher on that hill', and in a moment the slave appears *Above*. On the other hand, for the highway robbery in I HENRY IV it is the level Stage which is transformed into a hill—the 'uneven ground' so tormenting to the labouring Falstaff—by the skilfully placed words of the playwright and the gait of the players.

In the episode of Dover Cliff in KING LEAR the Poet's Method is at its subtlest: by poetical means we in the audience are fully persuaded that the blind Gloucester feels himself to have laboured to the top of that high and bending cliff; and yet we know 'the ground is even'.

In the matter of the grouping and movement of the players (of fundamental importance to the visual effect of the performance in a playhouse which knows nothing of naturalistic scenery) the stage-directions of the early texts are unhelpful; we are offered none of those precise instructions for the deployment of the actors on the stage that appear in the acting-editions of modern plays. We are not told whether an entrance should be made by the right or left Door, or through the curtains of the Study.[13] A differentiation, however, of the direction of exits or entrances is often explicitly required in the dialogue ('Go you down that way towards the Capitol, This way will I . . .') or stage-directions (*Enter a Fairie at one doore, and Robin goodfellow at another*). Indeed, the sequence in which the means of access to the Stage are used is implicit in the logic of the narrative; in the episode of Duncan's murder, for instance, the audience associates one entrance with the way to the King's bedchamber, another with the private apartment of Macbeth and his wife (in this direction they hastily retire when they hear the knocking at the gate), and a third, the Door by which the Porter admits Macduff, with the outside world—through it Malcolm and Donalbain, at the end of the scene, escape to safety. In the play-house, the sequence by which the logic of the narrative is maintained in the direction of exit and entrance sometimes makes it possible for the poet to create a strong sense of an immediate locality off-stage: if, in the second scene of JULIUS CAESAR, it is the left Door by which Caesar and his followers first enter, they will make their processional way across the Stage and depart by the right Door: throughout the sequel, while Cassius tempts Brutus to conspiracy, we shall be acutely aware that the Games are in progress out of our sight beyond the right Door; it is from that direction that we shall hear the shouts that twice, from a distance, interrupt the scene; it is from there too that Caesar and his train will reappear when 'The Games are done'; and when Casca describes the strange events that took place just out of our sight, the fact that we associate them with a clearly defined direction will help to create the sense of an objective reality in the mind's eye which is part of the playwright's purpose.

Only occasionally in the stage-directions of the early texts is there a recognition in general terms of the relationship between the grouping of the players and the structure of the scene—as, for instance, in the first Capitol scene of CORIOLANUS, where in the presence of the Senators the Tribunes are directed to *take their places by themselves*, while *Coriolanus stands*. Yet much may be deduced from a careful examination of the plays themselves: the movement of the players is often embodied in the words, or implicit in the interplay of action and mood. We may be sure that the ritualistic ceremony of the preparations for the contest of honour in the third scene of RICHARD II was given visible expression by the formal grouping of the King, the Lord Marshal and the rival Appellants, each with his own Herald. Much more complex are the demands of that long episode in JULIUS CAESAR which begins with Caesar's second encounter with the Soothsayer, his meeting with Artemidorus, and the panic-stricken reaction of the conspirators, continues through the murder of Caesar and the flight of people and Senators, to the ritual blooding of the assassins, their temporary reconciliation with Antony, his soliloquy of revenge and, finally, the colloquy of Antony and the Servant of Octavius. The scene proceeds from ceremony to disorder to ritual; a single player or group is detached from the rest for a moment; the focus of attention moves rapidly from player to player; above all, close analysis of the scene will show how often, and how positively, the movement of the players is embodied in the words they speak, whether they describe others ('Look how he makes to Caesar . . .') or themselves ('As low as to thy foot doth Cassius fall . . .'); only, as we have seen, for the murder itself must we rely upon a stage-direction alone.

In the consideration of grouping we must once again beware of the temptation to reduce Shakespeare's practice to standardised formula; a full analysis of the plays in performance will show how complex and various his practice is; and it is improbable that he would have made such demands if his fellows (in spite of the difficulties of rehearsal and performance inherent in the crowded routine of their professional life) could not fulfil them. However if, in our analysis, we keep constantly in mind the conditions for which Shakespeare wrote, we shall again and again find evidence of the poet's method at work—even, or perhaps especially, in those episodes of exciting action which seem to be primarily designed for the eyes of the audience; we shall see how often the movement of the players, the nature of the action, is contained in the words, interpreted through them, enriched by them. Each step in the duel between Hamlet and Laertes, for instance, is identified in the words the players speak; only for the turning-point itself must we rely on the Folio's stage-direction, *In scuffling they change Rapiers*: yet while we must see the action to understand why the duel has changed character, the change itself is at once interpreted for us in the words: 'Part them, they are incens'd. . . . They bleed on both sides.' Similarly, examination of the episodes of the blinding of Gloucester, the murder of Banquo, the gulling of Malvolio, the robbery at Gad's Hill, the attempted murder of Cassio, will be rewarding in its revelation of the poet's method. In each case, while we must see the action in order to understand it, our understanding is skilfully directed in the words the players speak.

It should not be surprising, then, that in the words of Shakespeare's dialogue we find many 'stage-directions' identifying and describing the appearance, gesture or movement of the players; through these words the action is not only described, but also given a particular dramatic colour. Some are direct, rather than implied, as this from MUCH ADO ABOUT NOTHING:

> For look where Beatrice like a Lapwing runs
> Close by the ground . . .

It is from Ariel's account subsequent to the event that we discover how Shakespeare intended his fellows to interpret in their demeanour the scene where Stephano and his gang hear the invisible music of pipe and tabor:

> . . .then I beat my Tabor,
> At which like unback'd colts they prick'd their ears,
> Advanc'd their eyelids, lifted up their noses
> As they smelt music . . .

The way in which, with innocent affection, Hermione takes the hand
of Polixenes, smiles at him, and looks up into his face, is not only
prescribed in the words of the observing Leontes, but coloured through
the medium of his diseased jealousy:

> But to be paddling Palms, and pinching Fingers,
> As now they are, and making practis'd Smiles
> As in a Looking-Glass . . .
> > Still Virginalling
> Upon his Palm? . . .
> How she holds up the Neb, the Bill to him!

Sometimes, however, action is implicit, rather than positively described, in the words. When Lear wakes out of his madness, Cordelia
speaks to him; she asks him to turn towards her:

> O look upon me Sir,
> And hold your hand in benediction o'er me . . .

She is a daughter asking the blessing of her father; the clear implication
of her words is that she kneels to him; and then she continues,

> You must not kneel.

A little emphasis on the pronoun 'you' makes the point: she kneels to
him, and he to her; it is a touching visual embodiment of their reconciliation, remembered later in the play when Lear imagines their
life together in prison:

> When thou dost ask me blessing, I'll kneel down
> And ask of thee forgiveness.

In the same play, the sudden first appearance of the almost naked
Edgar upon the heath is a *coup de théâtre* of a strikingly visual kind;
and yet its effect is due not only to the visual fact of his disguise: we
have been carefully prepared for it in his own soliloquy, when he tells
us that he will

with presented nakedness out-face
The Winds, and persecutions of the sky . . .

Just before Edgar's irruption on to the Stage, Lear remembers with
self-questioning compassion the

Poor naked wretches, wheresoe'er you are
That bide the pelting of this pitiless storm . . .

And Edgar's nakedness is explicitly presented to us, in the words of the
old King, as a visible token of humanity reduced to its essential nature:

Thou art the thing itself; unaccommodated man, is no more but
such a poor, bare, forked Animal as thou art.

It is an instance of how the visual aspects of performance are 'vested
by Shakespeare with important significances; they are theme-bearers'.[14]
Upon occasion, it is Shakespeare's way to focus our attention with
particular intensity upon a single visible detail, invest it with special
significance in the dialogue and action of his play, and make it for a
time the centre of dramatic interest, the embodiment of the themes or
issues with which he is concerned. An example of this practice is his
use of the stocks which (by the humiliation of Kent) embody Regan's
insult to her father's majesty. In the scene of Richard the Second's
abdication, the defeated King offers Bolingbroke his Crown; for a
moment both the fallen Richard and his adversary have their hands
upon the Crown at the same time, and it becomes, as it were, a visible
metaphor, clearly pointed and interpreted in Richard's words:

Here Cousin, on this side my Hand, on that side thine.
Now is this Golden Crown like a deep Well,
That owes two Buckets, filling one another,
The emptier ever dancing in the air,
The other down, unseen, and full of Water:
That Bucket down, and full of Tears am I,
Drinking my Griefs, whilst you mount up on high.

Shakespeare's use of the visible metaphor is more striking still in the scene in which Macbeth rejoins his wife after the murder of Duncan. Close examination of this passage will show with what insistence the poet directs our eyes towards the bloody hands which are the symbol of inescapable guilt, and how the effect of his symbol grows in intensity, despite Lady Macbeth's contemptuous dismissal of its implications. This image, first presented to the physical eye of the audience, is firmly fixed by the poet in the mind's eye too; and we shall remember it later in the play when we see how vainly Lady Macbeth 'rubs her hands', and hear of Macbeth:

Now does he feel
His secret Murthers sticking on his hands . . .

If, then, we are to attempt an imaginative reconstruction of Shakespeare's plays in performance, it is important that we keep constantly in mind the visual effect. It is not difficult to remember that the colour of Othello, the girth of Falstaff, the contrast in stature and complexion between Hermia and Helena, are visible facts, constantly before the eyes of the audience; and if we do remember these things, we shall begin to understand how many of the poet's lines and phrases fulfil their purposed function. Many of the mocks in MUCH ADO ABOUT NOTHING come to fuller life, if we follow Baldwin in believing that the part of Benedick was first played by Pope and that the same actor was also Falstaff and Sir Toby Belch; the robust size of the actor seems to be the butt of many shafts of wit: 'he's a very valiant Trencherman, he hath an excellent stomach . . . he is no less than a stuff'd man . . . the fool will eat no supper that night . . . you have no stomach signior. . . .' Indeed, Pope's healthy embonpoint seems to provide Beatrice with her last joke of all: she tells Benedick she will marry him, '. . . partly to save your life, for I was told, you were in a consumption'. At the beginning of the second scene of THE WINTER'S TALE we see Leontes, Hermione and Polixenes together for the first time; Polixenes begins the dialogue:

Nine Changes of the Wat'ry-Star hath been
The Shepherd's Note, since we have left our Throne
Without a Burden . . .

It is only when we see, as a visible fact, that the Queen standing by
him is pregnant, close to the time of child-bearing, that we understand how these innocently euphuistic words may be food for the
irrational jealousy of Leontes: it is nine months since Polixenes ar-
rived in Sicilia. After the botched suicide of Mark Antony, the dying
General asks his soldiers to dispatch him; they refuse, and one of them,
Decretas, takes his sword as a token that will commend him to
Octavius Caesar. When we see, as a visible fact, that Decretas still
carries this naked and bloodied weapon, it will not seem implausible
that Caesar should interpret his sudden irruption into the Roman
camp as a threat, and we will hear in Caesar's words, first momentary
agitation, and then an imperious return to self-command:

Wherefore is that? And what art thou that dar'st
Appear thus to us?

Caesar's expressive 'thus' has a visible correlative in a gesture towards
the sword; indeed, Shakespeare's fellows would have understood how
often his use of the word 'thus' indicated the need for a particular
gesture of identification.

But it is a testimony to the effectiveness of the Poet's Method that
Shakespeare can also make us ignore or forget what we can see on the
Stage with the physical eye; while we watch his plays in his playhouse, our faculty of vision is selective. In just such a way, we have
already suggested, he requires us sometimes to see and sometimes not
to see the permanent physical features of the Stage and Tiring-House.
But the same truth holds good of temporary properties or furniture,
even after the poet has carefully directed our attention towards them.
In As You Like It, Amiens bids Duke Senior's followers 'cover the
while,' (that is, they are to prepare the Duke's banquet while Amiens
finishes his song) 'the Duke will drink under this tree. . . .' At the end of
the scene he tells us, 'I'll go seek the Duke, His banquet is prepar'd.'

The picnic remains in full view throughout the ensuing scene, perhaps beside one of the Posts, serving for the moment as 'this tree'. But we do not see it while we watch the distress of old Adam: ,

> Dear Master, I can go no further:
> O I die for food.

It is a bold challenge to the disbelief of the audience. No less bold is the confidence with which the poet asks us to forget the presence of Kent in the stocks while Edgar makes his secret escape. Most remarkable of all is the way in which Shakespeare embellishes, through the mind's eye of the audience, the flowery bed of the Fairy Queen, focuses our attention upon the lullaby that sends her to sleep on it, and then for nearly two hundred lines of the dialogue induces us to forget her continuing presence on the Stage.

MUSIC AND SOUND-EFFECTS

Just as Shakespeare was always ready to put to dramatic use the visual resources of his playhouse and his company, so too he did not hesitate to explore the possibilities of music and other sound-effects.[15] The stage-directions of the early texts are much fuller and more explicit in their instructions for the use of music than they are in the matter of costume, properties or the movement of the players, and a perusal of them demonstrates how strikingly Shakespeare differed (and he is not unique among his contemporaries in this) from modern writers of 'straight' plays, in both the frequency and the variety of his demands for music: hardly a play in the whole canon of his work is without music. This truth is the more striking when we realise that the stage-directions, full as they are, are not complete: the dialogue of JULIUS CAESAR, I.ii, for instance, explicitly demands music (so ceremoniously loud that the Soothsayer can at first hardly make himself heard), although none is prescribed by the stage-directions until the moment of Caesar's departure from the Stage. For plays with unusually elaborate requirements Shakespeare's company no doubt called upon the services of professional musicians, but the players themselves not seldom showed skill in music as well as in acting or speaking. Augustine Phillips was an expert musician; it was for him, according to Baldwin, that Shakespeare wrote the part of Cassius; the poet enjoyed perhaps a private irony when he made Caesar say of the character played by this actor-musician that 'He loves no Plays . . . he hears no Music'. Lowin's Iago was required to sing; the part of Feste exploited to the full Armin's expertise not only as actor and clown, but as singer as well; the boy Lucius, whose acting role in JULIUS CAESAR is not negligible, sings too, accompanying himself on, presumably, the lute. Indeed, Shakespeare often drew upon the particular skill in singing of the boys; Desdemona must sing, if not expertly, at least melodiously and with pathos, as must Ophelia—and the player for whom Shakespeare wrote the volatile part of Ariel must have been highly gifted. Music was heard frequently in Shakespeare's playhouse, and it was various in its range too, requiring the use of drums, trumpets, cornets and horns, flutes, pipes and hautboys, as well as lute and voice: this list is probably not comprehensive.

Moreover the music was heard from many different parts of the playhouse.[16] Singers and players, other than the regular acting members of the company, not infrequently appeared within sight of the audience, on the Stage itself; the sound could come from above, as, perhaps, when Glendower calls upon 'Musicians that . . . Hang in the Air a thousand Leagues from thence'; it could come from below, as when in ANTONY AND CLEOPATRA *Musicke of the Hoboyes is under the Stage*, and the listening sentries surmise that 'the God Hercules, whom Antony loved, Now leaves him'. Often, so the stage-directions prescribe or the dialogue implies, music is heard *within*, that is, off-stage; in these cases, no doubt, the direction of the sound was determined by the logic of the narrative.

In spite of the frequency with which Shakespeare uses music, it is most important to understand that 'incidental music', of the kind we are used to in the cinema today, is not a feature of his practice: the music is part of the play; it is heard on the stage; it is never a comment shared only by the dramatist and the audience to the exclusion of the persons of the play. Sometimes it is directly informative: the sound of drums was a recognisable sign of an approaching army or imminent battle; the *dead March* was no doubt an identifiably different sound. The music of trumpets helps to create that atmosphere of public ceremony so often required in the plays; but it was often informative too, in that a nice discrimination between the different kinds of fanfare enabled the audience to identify at once the degree or nature of ceremony in the scene: the *Sennet*, for instance, was used only for the greatest State occasions, like the conclusion of peace at the end of HENRY V. Not only the tone of the scene itself, but also the Sennet which begins it, tells us that Lear resigns his crown in the full panoply of royal council—it is no mere family conference. Trumpet-calls could be informative in more particular ways: the audience could distinguish at once between the *Retreat* which marked the defeat of Macbeth, and the *Flourish* which, immediately following it, told them of Malcolm's victory. With a little help from the players, trumpets could even recognisably identify particular persons: 'The Moor,' cries Iago, 'I know his Trumpet.' Gloucester recognises Cornwall's *Tucket*, and Regan recognises her sister's.

It need hardly be said, however, that the function of music in Shakespeare's playhouse was not wholly or primarily informative. Although it was never incidental (in the modern sense), it was often used for the purpose of creating atmosphere, whether to prepare the audience to see ghosts (as in JULIUS CAESAR), or to evoke a mood of love-sick languor (as at the beginning of TWELFTH NIGHT). Drums and trumpets not only inform us of the approach of battle; they also help us to feel a sense of violent urgency or of heroic grandeur. The *Hornes* which herald the hunting-party of Theseus and, later, wake the sleeping lovers also reinforce the poet's words in dispelling the long night from the Athenian wood; *hornes in a peale* also suggest, but with grim irony (in view of the hideous sequel), a fragrant spring morning in TITUS ANDRONICUS. Especially beautiful in the harmonising of its appeal to the eye and the ear is the last scene of THE WINTER'S TALE: the poet requires that 'all stand still. . . . No foot shall stir', and in the hushed silence it is to the sound of music, commanded by Paulina, that the statue of Hermione begins at last to move with (so we feel from the gently repeated insistence of Paulina's entreaty) magical slowness. The harmonious formality of the end of AS YOU LIKE IT is conveyed partly in the *Still Musicke* which accompanies the entrance of Rosalind and Celia with Hymen. Music is indeed a symbol of the perfection of the natural order—it is the symbol used in speech by Lorenzo, by Exeter in HENRY V, and by Ulysses in TROILUS AND CRESSIDA—and not only in AS YOU LIKE IT and THE WINTER'S TALE does the sound of music in the playhouse become the expression of restored harmony; such a restoration, temporary though it is, is conveyed in the music which wakes the mad Lear to sanity; the measures of the dance which rocks the weary lovers to sleep in A MIDSUMMER NIGHT'S DREAM also tell us that 'all things shall be peace', the lovers reconciled, and Oberon and Titania new in amity.

Song in Shakespeare's plays, as well as instrumental music, is closely woven into the dramatic texture. This truth is evident even in the earlier plays, where the songs, though formally introduced, are appropriate to mood and situation; and as Shakespeare's mastery of his art developed, it became more so, as we see in the fragmented snatches of Ophelia and Desdemona and Lear's Fool, and in the songs of Ariel and the Goddesses in THE TEMPEST; they are an important part of the structure of image and idea in the play. It is not surprising that the poet-dramatist should put the words of his songs to dramatic effect— for Ferdinand it is the words of 'Full fathom five' that 'remember my drown'd father', and its coral, pearls and ringing bells are part of the imaginative world of the play. Amiens in As YOU LIKE IT sings of 'the green wood tree' and of 'Winter and rough Weather', of the 'winter wind', the 'bitter sky' and 'man's ingratitude' as well as of 'This Life' that is 'most jolly'; the songs express not only the background of rejection and exile in the wintry forest, but also the Duke's philosophical acceptance which tells him that 'Sweet are the uses of adversity'; and at the end of the play it is the words of the Pages' song that help to evoke in the playhouse the returning spring-time which brings the fulfilment of love. But the music no less than the words of the songs is at the service of the poet's purpose. Even where the settings have not survived, we may sometimes see how carefully the playwright calculated the dramatic effect of the music itself. Orsino prefers the 'old and plain' song of 'Come away, come away death' to the 'light airs . . . Of these most brisk and giddy-paced times'. That he does so is an ironic comment on his own changeable fancy; but the song is directly expressive of the simple truth of Viola's unswerving love—and it is before we have heard the words, while the tune is playing, that her own comment points this expressive effect: the music 'gives a very echo to the seat Where love is thron'd'. Just before the appearance of Caesar's Ghost, when the audience is hushed into silence by the song of Lucius, it is the effect of the music rather than the words which Brutus identifies for us: 'This is a sleepy Tune: O Murd'rous slumber!' The purpose of Balthasar's song in MUCH ADO ABOUT NOTHING is mischievously ironic: the music serves not only as the food of love for Claudio but also as a presage of Benedick's imminent fate; and it is on the melting tune, before he hears the deliberately conventional words, that Benedick with unconscious irony comments: 'Now divine air, now is his soul ravish'd, is it not strange that sheep's guts should hale souls out of men's bodies?'

But Shakespeare's plays demand a great variety of sound-effects other than music. Thunder, the Alarums of battle, the *noise of a Sea-fight* in ANTONY AND CLEOPATRA, the clatter of horses' hooves (whether galloping, trotting, coming to a halt, going about, or restlessly pacing in a stable-yard), the sounds of a banquet off-stage, the cry of the owl, the crowing of the cock, the gobble of turkeys, clocks, bells, hounds and larks—these and many other sounds either are specified in the stage-directions or can be deduced from the dialogue. Inevitably the purpose of many of these is to provide, with economy, information for the audience—of activity off-stage, for instance, or the time of day. But it should not surprise us that they are often atmospheric in their effect too. The poet conveys to his audience a sense of the passing of time in many different ways: the sound of a clock striking may project a feeling of sudden urgency or of clinching finality: after his rapt observation of the sleeping Imogen, Iachimo suddenly realises that the night is passing and he must 'To th'Trunk again'; and then the *Clocke strikes*, and he counts the chime: 'One, two, three: time, time.' His treacherous business is concluded. When the conspirators first meet in Brutus's orchard, their words convey to us the coming dawn of the day of Caesar's murder; towards the end of their conference a *Clocke strikes*, and, counting the strokes, they know ' 'Tis time to part'; the fulfilment of their murderous purpose seems very close as we hear 'The morning comes upon us. . . .' An important element in Shakespeare's (or Iago's) creation of a sense of turbulent disorder after the brawl of Cassio and Roderigo is the tolling of the tocsin, the insistent background to the agitated speech of the officers until Othello commands, 'Silence that dreadful Bell, it frights the Isle . . .'; and it is in a sudden silence that he begins his interrogation: 'What is the matter, Masters?' Quite different, but no less powerful in effect, are the two strokes of the bell which bring Macbeth to the point of murder: 'I go, and it is done: the Bell invites me. . . .' A whole chapter could be devoted to Shakespeare's use of the sound of thunder—sometimes to evoke storm and tempest, sometimes with special connotations of super-natural wickedness or moral disorder—in JULIUS CAESAR, MACBETH, THE WINTER'S TALE, OTHELLO and THE TEMPEST. Especially remark-able is that integration of sound-effects with the words of the poet which in the storm-sequence of KING LEAR evokes, as no naturalistic downpour can, a tempest both particular and universal, both physical and spiritual.

We must never forget that when the poet calls for music or other sound-effects, they become part of his score, that orchestration of words and sound by which he appeals through the ear to the mind's eye. Often the sound-effects seem to have a double effect—they fulfil their own informative or atmospheric purpose, and at the same time point or clinch, in the exact calculation of their timing, the words of the players on the stage. In KING LEAR (II.iv.129 ff.) the self-command of the old King gradually turns, under the bland taunting of his daughter Regan, to impotent rage; it is a swift and close-knit verbal crescendo, reaching a climax in her sharp command that he keep to the point, and in the fury of his reaction:

—Good Sir, to th'purpose.
—Who put my man i'th'Stocks?

And instantly, pointing this verbal climax, and topping it, we hear the *Tucket within* which announces the arrival of Goneril. The purpose of an off-stage Alarum of battle is primarily informative, but it may also sometimes have this same effect of pointing the poet's words. Twice during the battle of Philippi (throughout this sequence the sound-effects are calculated with exact care) *Low Alarums* not only remind us that in the distance the battle still continues, but also add their remote and sinister comment to the poet's words. The first is when the death of Cassius conjures up in the imagination of Brutus the ghostly presence of Caesar:

O Julius Caesar, thou art mighty yet,
Thy Spirit walks abroad, and turns our Swords
In our own proper Entrails.   *Low Alarums.*

88

And the second is when, to his schoolfellow Volumnius, Brutus admits the irrevocability of defeat:

Thou seest the World, Volumnius, how it goes,
Our Enemies have beat us to the Pit . . .   *Low Alarums.*

Conversely, although it is not an invariable rule, the sound-effects are often embodied in, interpreted through, enriched by the words of the players; this is not a matter of tautological information or mere decoration: it is through the poet's method that the playwright achieves his effect. An off-stage explosion is always effective in the theatre; how much more so it is in the hands of the poet may be seen from the third Chorus of HENRY V:

. . . the nimble Gunner
With Linstock now the devilish Cannon touches
                    Alarum, and Chambers goe off.
And down goes all before them.

In CORIOLANUS we hear the *Trumpets, Hoboyes, Drums beate, altogether* to welcome Volumnia back to the city she has saved from destruction; it is itself a merry noise, but it is through the words of an unnamed Messenger that the poet invests it with a special splendour:

. . . Why hark you:
The Trumpets, Sack-buts, Psalteries, and Fifes,
Tabors, and Cymbals, and the shouting Romans,
Make the Sun dance. Hark you.

In ANTONY AND CLEOPATRA the distant drums which tell us that in the early dawn the Roman camp is stirring, also quietly mark the death of Enobarbus; and the dual effect is expressed in the words of the sentry:

The hand of death hath raught him.
                    Drummes afarre off.
Hark the Drums demurely wake the sleepers . . .

Through the interpretative words of the players the sound-effects may serve thus not only the playwright's immediate dramatic purpose, but also his long-range strategy, as when, in the words of the imprisoned Richard the Second, music (so often the symbol of order) becomes the symbol of his destruction of the concord of his time and state. To Alonso, the strange sounds he has heard are reminders of his guilt, and as he thus interprets them they become part of the pervasive imagery of the play:

> Methought the billows spoke, and told me of it,
> The winds did sing it to me: and the Thunder
> (That deep and dreadful Organ-Pipe) pronounc'd
> The name of Prosper: it did bass my Trespass . . .

The effect of the most famous of all Shakespeare's off-stage sounds, the knocking on the gate in MACBETH, is the greater because it is the climax of a long sequence (beginning with Macbeth's plea to the Earth itself, 'Hear not my steps . . .') in which the playwright, partly through the use of other sound-effects, but mostly through the themes and images conveyed in the words of the players, focuses the attentive imagination of his audience upon the act of listening in the hushed and sleeping house. When we understand how often and how skilfully music and other sound-effects are integrated into Shakespeare's dramatic texture, we begin to see how easily the use of extraneous sounds which did not enter into his conception, or of incidental music (however tactful), or of music which is anachronistically unsuitable to the world of Shakespeare's playhouse, may disturb the carefully organised balance of his plays.

THE TEXT

In our attempt to envisage the performances of Shakespeare's day, we have deliberately eschewed fashions of music and costume of later periods. It is no less important that the text we use as our prompt-book should introduce no anachronisms of theatrical practice. The material is available in sufficient quantity; for apart from the eighteen or so plays of which there exist separate Quarto texts published in Shakespeare's lifetime (pages which he himself possibly, indeed probably, perused with his own eye), there are other plays in Quarto, and the First Folio collected edition of 1623 (not to mention the Second Quarto of 1632) which were published before the closure of the theatres in 1642; all these, in some degree, reflect (in spite of erratic copyists and the vagaries of the printing-house) stage-practice in the conditions of the playhouse which we are studying and which we may call Shakespeare's own. The quality of the Quarto texts, as the textual scholars have shown us, is uneven. Most of them record, at various removes, Shakespeare's own manuscript (known technically as the 'foul papers') or the transcribed prompt-books from which the actors worked in the playhouse. The unique importance of the First Folio lies partly in the fact that it was presented to the world by two of Shakespeare's fellow-actors, John Heminges and Henry Condell, two of the people who knew him best. It was long the custom of scholars to decry their edition, but Greg showed that they, and the anonymous literary editor who probably helped them, were careful and devoted in their work, and succeeded, as far as the material available to them allowed, in their aim of publishing the plays 'according to the True Original Copies'. Modern editors can do no better than subscribe to this high aim of Shakespeare's colleagues, while echoing the wish expressed with humility in their preface, 'that the Author himself had liv'd to have set forth, and overseen his own writings'.

In considering separate plays, we shall have to work on the basis of the original texts, whether Quarto or Folio or both, in the light of the findings of the textual scholars.[17] What is important for our express purpose is the plain fact that the compilers of these first texts were working mainly from playhouse documents (at first or further remove) and were for the most part little concerned with the practice of literary criticism or the rules of textual emendation and elucidation, now formulated as an exact science. It is worth remembering that Heminges and Condell would be recollecting the plays as performances in which they were used to taking part. We have in these early texts, therefore, if we can interpret them aright, a wealth of information about what actually happened in Shakespeare's playhouse.

It will be as well to state in general terms some of the ways in which a study of the Quarto and Folio texts can help our investigation:

(1) The *Title-Pages* of the Quarto texts are important for various reasons. We can learn from the simple statement that A MIDSUMMER NIGHT'S DREAM was 'sundry times pub*lickely acted, by the Right honour-able, the Lord Chamberlaine his servants*', or that 'The Tragoedy of Othello, the Moore of Venice' was '*diverse times acted at the* Globe, and at the Black Friers, by *his Majesties Servants.*' There is a hint of theatrical emphasis in the description of 'The Cronicle History of Henry the fift, With his battell fought at *Agin Court* in *France*. Togither with *Auntient Pistoll.*' Highly informative is the title-page to the 1608 Quarto of the 'True Chronicle Historie of the life and death of King LEAR and his three Daughters. *With the unfortunate life of* Edgar, *sonne* and heire to the Earle of Gloster, and his sullen and assumed humor of TOM of Bedlam.' This title seems to show that, in Shakespeare's conception, the courageous, resourceful, compassionate Edgar (not the plausible, self-seeking opportunist Edmund) is the focal figure of his sub-plot.

(2) The *Continuity* of the plays, as recorded in almost all the Quartos, is uninterrupted. A general *Exeunt* is the only mark of the end of a scene, and is followed (with scarcely more than the normal gap that indicates in a prose text a new paragraph) by a new entry. This reflects the practice of continuous performance in the theatre, described in simile in RICHARD II.* The marking of Act and Scene in the Folio

* See *page 45, above.*

is often so incomplete and rudimentary as to give the impression that such divisions were in the main an uncharacteristic attempt on the part of the editors to lend the volume a literary flavour, though Dover Wilson has suggested that they may reflect the practice of the Black-friars rather than the Globe. While we do not wish to imply that breaks in the action were wholly unknown in Shakespeare's playhouse, we cannot neglect the dramatic effect of immediate sequence between scenes, which is especially important because of Shakespeare's habit of insistent relevance in narrative. We have already noticed the ironical juxtaposition of KING JOHN, IV.ii and iii.* Such dramatic use of sequence is a commonplace of Shakespeare's writing. Macbeth, hearing that Macduff is 'fled to England', cries:

> The Castle of Macduff, I will surprise,
> Seize upon Fife; give to th'edge o'th'Sword
> His Wife, his Babes, and all unfortunate Souls
> That trace him in his Line.

Four lines later, *Enter Macduffes Wife, her Son, and Rosse.* When at the end of this scene (probably taking place above, in the Chamber) Lady Macduff runs off *crying Murther*, and her cries are suddenly silenced in death, *Enter Malcolme and Macduffe*, on the Stage below; and Macduff describes how

> each new Morn,
> New Widows howl, new Orphans cry, new sorrows
> Strike heaven on the face . . .

The battle-sequences are notable examples: the 'excursions' of actual combat are secondary to the points of dramatic emphasis sharply out-lined in the rapid succession of significant incidents. In the last Act of KING JOHN, the presentation of the battle is built round the King's sickness and retirement to Swinsted, Melun's dying confession which stirs the English 'Revolts' to return to their own side, and the Dolphin's reception of the news of their falling off and the wreck of his supply

* See *page 45, above.*

on the Goodwin Sands. Shrewsbury Field, the climax of I HENRY IV, is a tour-de-force of construction, which depends for its effect upon the swift succession of events and moods. The three-day battle in ANTONY AND CLEOPATRA is unintelligible unless it is presented with the continuity which is native to the Elizabethan playhouse, and which is reflected in the Folio's presentation, episode after episode flowing uninterrupted by any suggestion of locality: indeed, after an initial concession to literary etiquette (*Actus Primus. Scoena Prima.*), the play is printed without division from start to finish.[18]

(3) The *Punctuation* of the early texts needs careful consideration. Percy Simpson's pioneering work first drew attention to the view that the punctuation was less an aid (like modern pointing) to understanding the syntax of a sentence, than a guide to how the sentence should be delivered. No one approaching this study should omit to read and re-read Chambers's cautionary pages in which we are warned against discovering any regular system or any clear distinction between 'logical' and 'rhetorical' punctuation. Dr. Richard Flatter's chapter on the punctuation of the Folio text, while seeming to agree with Chambers in his admission that 'even if we restrict our investigation to those plays of which we may assume with any measure of probability that they show at least partly Shakespeare's own punctuation we might still find it difficult to make out any cut and dried system in it', nevertheless quotes many convincing examples of punctuation which gives a clue to the actor of how he should speak a line. In a positive and fruitful discussion, M. R. Ridley comes to the conclusion 'that in the punctuation of the early texts we have, pretty certainly, at least "playhouse" punctuation, and very possibly a great deal of Shakespeare's own. If this is so,' he adds, 'it means that no modern editor can neglect the Q and F punctuation.' It is self-evident that neither should a modern director or actor do so. And since we are on the quest of what happened in Shakespeare's playhouse, we too shall give due weight to this part of the evidence.[19]

Playhouse scribes, 'editors' whether from among Shakespeare's player-colleagues or his more 'literary' acquaintance, and the compositors themselves with their printing-house conventions, have all had a hand in distributing the punctuation of the early texts, which cannot therefore be said to represent with any certainty the author's own marks. Moreover where a single play appears in both Quarto and Folio, the punctuation of the two versions is not always the same. But we should keep two considerations in mind; first, that these texts are the nearest we have to Shakespeare's intentions, and for the lack of other contemporary evidence, we should begin with them; and secondly, that (in spite of the unreliability of individual compositors) they generally represent methods of pointing which were thought acceptable in Shakespeare's day, whether for syntax, logic or rhetoric.

That Shakespeare was fully aware of a relation between punctuation and intelligible speaking, we know from the notorious Prologue of Peter Quince, and the comments of Duke Theseus and Lysander:

—This fellow doth not stand upon points.
—He hath rid his Prologue, like a rough Colt: he knows not the stop. A good moral my Lord. It is not enough to speak, but to speak true.

And if the craftsmen of the printing-house were capable of recording with flawless accuracy the deliberate mis-pointing of Quince's Prologue, they were surely able to observe the author's intentions elsewhere. Besides, in the midst of much inconsistency some features are most consistently regular: for instance, the presence or absence of the apostrophe ('d) of the past tense is an almost infallible clue to the rhythm of a line. In a familiar passage of A MIDSUMMER NIGHT'S DREAM, the 'faire Vestall' is 'throned by the West', her assailant 'loos'd his love-shaft smartly from his bow', young Cupid's fiery shaft is 'Quencht in the chaste beams of the watry Moone';

And the imperiall Votresse passed on,
In maiden meditation, fancy free.

The key-words for the rhythm are the same in both Quarto and Folio: 'throned . . . loos'd . . . Quencht . . . passed. . . .' So likewise, the dis-syllables 'watry' and 'Votresse' are clearly indicated. We should also understand that, from their long experience of acting in the plays,

Heminges and Condell, the editors of the Folio, would be likely to remember through the ear rather than visually from the written page. Certainly, the memory of Kemp's phrasing seems to echo through their printing of those set-pieces which he made famous—Launce's unilateral conversations with Crab, 'the sourest natured dog that lives', Launcelot Gobbo's three-part dialogue between the cross-fire of the Devil and his Conscience, Dogberry's cadenza of outraged dignity, a torrent scarcely checked by the weak commas until it is dammed at its height by two indignant colons:

> ... I am a wise fellow, and which is more, an officer, and which is more, a householder, and which is more, as pretty a piece of flesh as any in Messina, and one that knows the Law, go to, and a rich fellow enough, go to, and a fellow that hath had losses, and one that hath two gowns, and every thing handsome about him: bring him away: O that I had been writ down an ass!

George Sampson in the introduction to his school-text of ROMEO AND JULIET (10 f.) states the case with his habitual plain speaking: 'That the old punctuation sometimes divides subject and predicate, and sometimes does not divide clauses, may offend grammar but does not offend sense. The punctuation of a dramatic text should indicate how it should be spoken, not how it should be parsed.' Among the examples he quotes is Juliet's impatient line, which is printed in a modern edition thus:

> Nay, come, I pray thee, speak; good, good nurse, speak!

For this the Folio has:

> Nay come I pray thee speak, good good Nurse speak.

Sampson adds, 'it is obvious that, for dramatic purposes, the original punctuation is more simple, more sensible and more speedy than the modern. Its supreme merit is that it imposes no check on the natural fluency of speech.' It may be said in this connection that, more often than not, the Folio has no comma before the vocative address: Cordelia says 'Nothing my Lord', Lear silences interruption with 'Peace Kent . . .', Kent's parting speech, as he goes into banishment, begins 'Fare thee well King. . . .' This is the natural fluency of speech, the rule rather than the exception: it is when we find otherwise, that we should seek a special reason—Lear's sarcastic challenge to Goneril, 'Your name, fair Gentlewoman?' and his extravagant courtesy to the naked Bedlam philosopher, 'Come, good Athenian', are interesting examples of a different and deliberate pointing: in each case the vocative is surprising and demands unusual emphasis from the player. Every speech, each sentence, each phrase must be weighed in its context of sense and mood and situation. We want to know how they sounded when they were first delivered in Shakespeare's playhouse.[20] For this purpose we cannot neglect the clues, although they may not always be trustworthy, which survive in the early printed texts.

For a specimen, the reader is recommended to speak aloud (with the punctuation of the Folio) Cleopatra's speech as she prepares to take her life 'after the high Roman fashion':

> Give me my Robe, put on my Crowne, I have
> Immortall longings in me. Now no more
> The juyce of Egypts Grape shall moyst this lip.
> Yare, yare, good *Iras*; quicke: Me thinkes I heare
> *Anthony* call: I see him rowse himselfe
> To praise my Noble Act. I heare him mock
> The lucke of *Caesar*, which the Gods give men
> To excuse their after wrath. Husband, I come:
> Now to that name, my Courage prove my Title.
> I am Fire, and Ayre; my other Elements
> I give to baser life. So, have you done?
> Come then, and take the last warmth of my Lippes.
> Farewell kinde *Charmian*, *Iras*, long farewell.
> Have I the Aspicke in my lippes? Dost fall?
> If thou, and Nature can so gently part,
> The stroke of death is as a Lovers pinch,
> Which hurts, and is desir'd.

The highly dramatic rhythm of this speech is unmistakable in the punctuation and lineation of the printed text. There can be no question of a compositor's whim in the exact calculation of stop against stop.

Significant too is the use of *Capital Letters*, as this passage from AN-TONY AND CLEOPATRA shows, in giving weight to a word in its context. We must again be aware of Chambers's warning against assuming that there is any uniformity of capitalisation: 'Of course many of the words are important, but it is rather an exaggeration to speak of "emphasis-capitals".' Nevertheless, though they cannot be analysed to represent a system of emphasis, the Folio's capitals seem to reflect from time to time a sense of thematic proportion. Certainly the incidence of these capitals is not haphazard, dependent on the choice of the compositor or some purely accidental and mechanical cause. A habit of mind, however inconsistent, seems to underlie them—whether they preserve Shakespeare's intention, or that of his two editors, or the recollection of the practice of their fellow-actors. Often the purpose seems clear, to underline the sense, as for instance in the passage of Hamlet's advice to the Players (quoted on *page 54, above*), where the salient points are scrupulously marked with capitals: '... Discretion ... Tutor ... Action ... Word ... Word ... Action ... Nature ... Playing ... Mirror ... Nature.' The first time that we in the audience hear of the existence of Lady Macbeth is marked by an expressive comma in the Folio text. When King Duncan invites himself to Inverness to show his esteem for his general's prowess in battle, Macbeth's words are thus printed:

> Ile be my selfe the Herbenger, and make joyfull
> The hearing of my Wife, with your approach ...

Both the capital letter for 'Wife' and the following comma serve to lay dramatic emphasis on the first introduction of this baleful protagonist to our notice.

It is for reasons such as these that, in quoting, we have made a practice of reproducing, as far as possible without obscuring the sense, the Folio's punctuation and capital letters, so that the reader may have the means of deciding for himself the degree of their significance in each instance. Occasionally, for his convenience, we have made changes so as to avoid a serious confusion, and indeed have modernised the spelling throughout.

(4) Equally important is the problem of *Lineation*. It should be clear that Shakespeare, although taking the iambic pentameter as his norm of verse-writing, used an infinite variety of speech-rhythms to give life to his dialogue. The attempt to fit his verses into the strait-jacket of regularity began with the post-Restoration editors. It is true that curiosities of lineation are sometimes caused by the incompetence of the printers or (in the case of the Folio) by the problems of type-setting by formes.[21] Nevertheless, irregular lineation often represents the poet's eloquent counterpoint to the regular pentameter.

One example out of many will make the point clear. The Folio version of MACBETH, II.i.12–17, runs as follows:

What Sir, not yet at rest? the King's a bed.
He hath beene in unusuall Pleasure,
And sent forth great Largesse to your Offices.
This Diamond he greetes your Wife withall,
By the name of most kind Hostesse,
And shut up in measurelesse content.

A typical modern edition prints it thus:

What, sir, not yet at rest? The King's abed:
He hath been in unusual pleasure, and
Sent forth great largess to your offices:
This diamond he greets your wife withal,
By the name of most kind hostess; and shut up
In measureless content.

In the modern version, the moment's telling pause at the end of the second line is lost. The Folio's third line makes a natural elision of 'to your', and distributes the emphasis where it is wanted: in the modern text the word 'to' has more weight than it can conveniently bear. The penultimate line in the modern text has become hurried and clumsy. The Folio lineation suggests that the last two lines of the speech must be spoken very slowly; the words 'most kind' and 'shut up' are the most leisurely of all, each word occupying the space of a whole iambic foot. Thus the lines each contain the normal five stresses, and the atmosphere of drowsy contentment is emphasised.

Another problem of lineation is caused by the rhythmical relation of one speaker's words to another's. There is only one modern popular edition, to our knowledge, which preserves that almost invariable practice of the compositors of Quartos and Folio, by which every new speech is printed close to the speech-heading of the speaker. This is G. B. Harrison's edition of the original Penguin Shakespeare, now superseded by the new Penguin series which unhappily reverts to the traditional practice of attempting a division of lines by indentation. The fact is that Shakespeare employed a fluidity of rhythm which any such indentation must obscure or restrict. Two examples will indicate the dilemma.

Hamlet is questioning Horatio, Barnardo and Marcellus about the appearance of his father's Ghost. This is how a traditional text presents the dialogue:

Hamlet	Indeed, indeed, sirs, but this troubles me.
	Hold you the watch to-night?
Marcellus *Barnardo* }	We do, my lord.
Hamlet	Arm'd, say you?
Marcellus *Barnardo* }	Arm'd, my lord.
Hamlet	From top to toe?
Marcellus *Barnardo* }	My lord, from head to foot.
Hamlet	Then saw you not his face?
Horatio	O yes! my lord; he wore his beaver up.
Hamlet	What! look'd he frowningly?
Horatio	A countenance more in sorrow than in anger.
Hamlet	Pale or red?
Horatio	Nay, very pale.

Hamlet	And fix'd his eyes upon you?
Horatio	Most constantly.
Hamlet	I would I had been there.
Horatio	It would have much amaz'd you.
Hamlet	Very like, very like. Stay'd it long?
Horatio	While one with moderate haste might tell a hundred.
Marcellus *Barnardo*	}Longer, longer.
Horatio	Not when I saw it.
Hamlet	His beard was grizzled, no?
Horatio	It was, as I have seen it in his life, A sable silver'd.
Hamlet	I will watch to-night; Perchance 'twill walk again.
Horatio	I warrant it will.
Hamlet	If it assume my noble father's person, I'll speak to it, though hell itself should gape, And bid me hold my peace.

Nothing is surer than that Hamlet's questions are agitated, and appropriately extra-metrical, until the moment when he makes up his mind: 'I will watch to-night.' From that point his words have a cogent rhythmical regularity. The answers of Horatio preserve, as far as possible, the metrical regularity of the anxiously sympathetic but positive witness. It is Horatio's function, over and over again during the play, to restrain the excesses of Hamlet's volatile temperament. The indentations of the modern text show in Hamlet an orderliness of conversation which is not Shakespeare's intention. Quarto and Folio print each speech close to the speech-heading.

A simpler example occurs in MACBETH, IV.iii.218 ff. Macduff, hearing of the slaughter of his family, cries:

What, All my pretty Chickens, and their Dam
At one fell swoop?

Malcolm continues his line—

> Dispute it like a man.

And Macduff retorts in the rhythm of Malcolm's half-line—

> (Dispute it like a man)—
>   I shall do so . . .

In this instance Malcolm's words are metrically joined to form a pentameter line both with what precedes and with what follows. The attempted indentation of modern editors obscures this eloquent rhythmical device. It is to preserve such calculated variations that a standard text should follow the general practice of the compositors of both Quartos and Folio, of printing the beginning of every speech close to the speech-heading. And in this respect G. B. Harrison's Penguin Shakespeare edition is preferable to all other popular modern texts.[22]

(5)   *Speech-headings* are also sometimes revealing, for they suggest how Shakespeare's mind may have worked as he conceived a character in his part in the play: it is as if sometimes the part he or she plays in the story is more to the fore in the poet's mind than the individual character: *Capulet* alternates with *Father*, *Lady Capulet* with *Mother*; *Armado* becomes *Braggart*, *Pedant* hits off *Holofernes*. It is true that variations in speech-headings may be simply the result of a particular compositor's whim, but even these in their own fashion represent a living view of the persons of the play. Occasionally indeed the compositor (or his copy) gives us a clue to the casting of the play, as when the speeches of Dogberry and Verges are ascribed in the 1600 Quarto of MUCH ADO ABOUT NOTHING to *Kemp* and *Cowley*.

(6)   As we have already seen, the *Stage-Directions* of the Quartos and Folio, although sometimes ambiguous or incomplete or contradictory, can help our enquiry in various ways. In the bulk of the texts they are few and mainly factual. It is to be presumed that as long as Shakespeare was working with his colleagues in the playhouse, full descriptive instructions in the prompt-book were unnecessary: it is noticeable that in the earliest plays of the canon, before he was fully established as a

regular playwright for the Chamberlain's Men, and again in the latest plays, when he was no longer actively participating in rehearsal, the instructions are more elaborate. However, throughout the canon there are directions which reveal momentary action, *Enter one blowing* for a messenger in a hurry to give sensational news; or the appearance of an actor, *Enter Cassandra with her haire about her eares*; or his demeanour, as when we are to see Alonso *with a franticke gesture*; or (as we have noted) the costume and make-up of an actor, *Enter Morochus a tawnie Moore all in white, and three or foure followers accordingly*; or the age of a character—Alice, Princess Katherine's attendant, is *an old Gentlewoman*; a whiff of patronage, *Enter young Osricke*, is appropriate for the callow 'waterflie'. Some examples give hints of the disposition of a scene on the multiple stage: the gulling of Christopher Sly, although it involves a number of players and some elaborate properties, seems to take place in the Chamber—*Enter aloft the drunkard with attendants, some with apparel, Bason and Ewer, & other appurtenances, & Lord*; a higher level still may be indicated by the direction *Prosper on the top (invisible)*; Hamlet's father's *Ghost cries under the Stage*. In ANTONY AND CLEOPATRA the company of soldiers on watch *place themselves in every corner of the Stage*, and are startled when they hear subterranean sounds: *Musicke of the Hoboyes is under the Stage*. Details of 'business' appear in CORIOLANUS, when we are told that the Ladies *set them downe on two lowe stooles and sowe*, and of the Plebeians that *They all shout, and throw up their Caps*. This play is full of elaborate descriptive directions, including the eloquent climax when, in answer to his mother's appeal, Coriolanus *Holds her by the hand silent*. Among the early plays, the text of TITUS ANDRONICUS is especially well equipped with detailed explanation of grouping and stage-business: the complicated instructions for the long first scene deserve close study. A representative selection of stage-directions from Quartos and Folio is given by Greg in *The Editorial Problem in Shakespeare* (158 ff.). The most cursory glance at this list evokes a series of vivid pictures in the mind's eye and brings us appreciably nearer in imagination to the atmosphere of rehearsal and performance in Shakespeare's playhouse.

(7) There are, of course, difficulties involved in the practice of working from the early texts. The problems raised by unfamiliar

conventions of presentation, spelling and punctuation are relatively simple of solution, but others require more careful consideration: there are inconsistencies of detail which manifestly need emendation; some passages seem to be corrupt; some look like interpolations by a hand other than Shakespeare's; some appear to be incomplete. Most interesting of all is the necessity for collation and comparison where a play exists in both Quarto and Folio texts. A glance at the New Cambridge and Arden editions of OTHELLO will indicate not only the nature and extent of the difficulties, but also the degree to which scholars may differ in their interpretations and conclusions in this matter of textual comparison.[23] Although the problem is mainly an editorial one, it is not irrelevant to our purpose of trying to reconstruct what actually happened in Shakespeare's playhouse. We have seen already, in the case of ROMEO AND JULIET, that both the dialogue and the stage-directions of two versions of the same scene may imply differences of stage practice.* If we are to reconstruct a performance of HAMLET in Shakespeare's playhouse, we must consider the fact that the Folio version is considerably shorter than the Second Quarto, and recognise the possibility that the 'cuts' may represent playhouse practice at some point in the early history of the play. Sometimes a change in speech-headings may seem to be significant: the descriptive lines, in HAMLET, IV.v, which first bring to our attention the madness of Ophelia are given in the Second Quarto to *a Gentleman* and in the Folio to Horatio; the change may recognise that particular skill in speaking is needed from the actor who thus directs our interpretation of the poor girl's distracted speech. It is even possible that reference to one of those 'stol'n, and surreptitious' versions of the plays which the Folio editors aimed to correct may help us in our search for a deeper understanding of Shakespeare's dramatic craftsmanship. The 'bad' First Quarto of HAMLET, travesty as it is of Shakespeare's play, may nevertheless be a reconstruction made by an eyewitness; if so, the details of action it records are significant, however untrustworthy its dialogue may be: the Ghost appears in Gertrude's closet dressed *in his night gowne*; in her madness Ophelia appears *playing on a Lute, and her haire downe singing*; these and other such details may help us to in-

* See *page* 39, *above*, and Note 4.

terpret the more trustworthy texts of the Second Quarto and Folio. When we are dealing with a play which appeared in one version only, our task is in many ways much easier; and yet another substantive text of MACBETH would have been helpful to us in our consideration of whether or not the Hecate passages are interpolations. In JULIUS CAESAR, which was printed only in the Folio edition, one speech (V.iv.7 f.) appears without a speech-heading: another substantive text would have helped us to decide whether to follow those editors who give the lines to Brutus or those who, remembering Plutarch's version of the story, give them to Lucilius.

In most modern editions of Shakespeare's plays the inconsistencies of the early texts are ironed out, and the difficulties of interpretation and comprehension solved for us; but we pay a price for this scholarly help in that our understanding of Shakespeare is subtly and pervasively directed by the editor: punctuation is modernised and lineation rational-ised; each scene opens with an identification of locality (*A lawn before the Duke's palace* or *The coast of Wales. A castle in view*) which carries us far from the flexible conditions for which Shakespeare wrote; and while stage-directions sometimes accurately pinpoint the implications of Shakespeare's text, at other times they impose an editorial interpreta-tion on the unwary reader. Above all, we must understand that the editorial purpose is, largely, a literary rather than a theatrical one, and while it is impossible to compute the huge debt we owe to that great line of editors from Theobald and Johnson to the scholars of our own time, we must regret too the distance they have brought us from Shakespeare's playhouse. We strongly urge interpreters of Shakespeare, player and student alike, to work from the early printed texts, which are readily available in facsimile. The quiddities of the Elizabethan and Jacobean printing-houses are no great obstacle to the judicious reader, and under the seemingly eccentric variations of spelling, punctuation, lineation, speech-headings, stage-directions, there lie many clues and trails for the detective who would unravel the mystery of what really happened on the stage of Shakespeare's playhouse.

THE SOURCES

The recognisable sources of Shakespeare's inspiration have been the subject of close and exhaustive study, chiefly for the purpose of exploring the poet's method of composition, the process from conception in the mind to the written page. The basic material is identified and selectively printed in the appendices to some editions of the plays, and is comprehensively available in Professor Bullough's monumental compilation and assessment of the *Narrative and Dramatic Sources of Shakespeare*. The varied process of Shakespeare's use of the material is most skilfully and luminously set forth in Kenneth Muir's *Shakespeare's Sources*, of which the first volume covers some twenty of the plays.[24]

We too shall make reference to this material, as one means of deducing why, in this passage or that, Shakespeare wrote as he did. That is a primary motive for comparing his work with the sources on which he drew. We can learn both from his close imitation and from his divergences from his sources. Such a comparison often shows how he deliberately altered the emphases of his source-story. Shakespeare's gentle Orlando, unlike his prototype in Lodge's *Rosalynde*, does not kill his opponent in the wrestling-ring. Holinshed's Banquo is implicated in Macbeth's treachery, his Duncan is no sainted king and his Macbeth, once in power, rules for a time well and justly. While in Plutarch the deserter Domitius is 'sicke of an agewe' at the moment of his leaving his master Antony, Shakespeare's Enobarbus dies of no other apparent cause than his grief and shame. Sometimes, while the source-book suggests the initial dramatic situation of a plot, Shakespeare's whole development of it is different. Greene's *Pandosto*, the source of THE WINTER'S TALE, ends as a tragedy of incest and suicide. The alterations that Shakespeare makes in the dénouement are not merely a last-minute change in the direction of the narrative, but colour the whole mood and feeling of the play. A comparison of the plays and their sources often shows us, too, how Shakespeare moulded desultory narrative into coherent dramatic form—for instance, by the transposition and alteration of scenes, by the development of passing hints and the elaboration of minor characters, by the contraction of lengthy episodes, by the skilful integration of different sources or different parts of the same source. It is matter of great interest to observe the particular means by which the poet, who from his earliest days as a playwright had so remarkable a sense of dramatic architecture, converted the sordid melodrama of Cinthio's ignoble tale into the heart-searching tragedy of OTHELLO. Such study bears chiefly upon the process of Shakespeare's composition—the poet's pen turning the hints and suggestions of his source into dramatic shapes upon the page—in solitary retreat or by the midnight oil.

We are concerned, however, with the busy day's work too, as the player-playwright and his colleagues translated the written word into histrionic action and visual and audible substance. And there are special ways in which this study of the sources can help our immediate purpose of reconstructing the plays in performance in Shakespeare's playhouse. We can best illustrate this approach by examples from his handling of North's Plutarch, the source which he followed most closely, both in framing the outline of his narrative and in the detail of his expression. It is plain that in Plutarch he recognised a kindred spirit, with a sense of the dramatic strong enough to stimulate his own.

(1) What did the Chamberlain's Men do at the moment of the assassination of Caesar? The Folio's stark direction informs us that *They stab Caesar*, and that he *Dyes*. From the two vivid accounts which Plutarch gives of this moment in history we can reconstruct a scene of great violence, a prolonged struggle. Metellus Cimber, who has been the first suitor, taking Caesar's gown 'with both his hands, pulled it over his neck, which was the sign given the confederates to set upon him'. Then follows Casca's blow from behind him on the neck. 'Howbeit the wound was not great nor mortal': so that Caesar 'feeling himself hurt, took him straight by the hand he held his dagger in'. Then the rest close in, so that 'Caesar turned him no where but he was stricken at by some, and still had naked swords in his face, and

was hackled and mangled among them, as a wild beast taken of hunters'. There is a moment when he finds himself confronted by 'Brutus with a sword drawn in his hand ready to strike at him.'

Et Tu Brute?——Then fall Caesar.

The rare long dash in the Folio text indicates the pause and the silence that follows his question: no doubt the other conspirators stay their hands for a while, to see what Brutus will do ('for it was agreed among them that every man should give him a wound'). At sight of Brutus, Caesar pulls his gown over his head. Brutus delivers his single blow. Thereafter Caesar 'made no more resistance, and was driven either casually or purposedly, by the counsel of the conspirators, against the base whereupon Pompey's image stood'. Clearly, on Shakespeare's stage, the assassins hustled their victim towards one of the Stage-Posts, and it was here at its base that Pompey's enemy yielded up the ghost. That it was with this or some such action that Burbage and Phillips and the rest disposed of old Heminges on the stage of the brand-new Globe in 1599, we may be sure, because the scene is described in two passages later in the play. The gown ('You all do know this Mantle') is made much of in Antony's funeral oration. Brutus's blow is 'the most unkindest cut of all':

> For when the Noble Caesar saw him stab,
> Ingratitude, more strong than Traitors' arms,
> Quite vanquish'd him: then burst his Mighty heart,
> And in his Mantle, muffling up his face,
> Even at the Base of Pompey's Statue
> (Which all the while ran blood) great Caesar fell.

So too, when before the battle of Philippi, the generals taunt each other in a cross-stage wrangle, Antony describes how

> your vile daggers
> Hack'd one another in the sides of Caesar:
> You show'd your teeth like Apes, and fawn'd like Hounds,

And bow'd like Bondmen, kissing Caesar's feet;
Whilst damned Casca, like a Cur, behind
Struck Caesar on the neck.

That some of the details of the historical account recur in these descriptions suggests that the whole action on Shakespeare's stage was modelled on Plutarch's narrative; and Plutarch's narrative reads almost like a set of stage-directions for Shakespeare's scene. A similarly violent scene of murder occurs in Holinshed's account of the miserable end of Richard the Second; once again Shakespeare's dialogue seems to spring directly from the elaborate action described in his source, and it seems likely that the Chamberlain's Men followed in their performance the directions implied in Holinshed.

(2) In JULIUS CAESAR too, the strange episode of Portia's voluntary wound has an immediacy in Plutarch's account which is not at once apparent on the printed page of Shakespeare's text. After a vividly detailed account of Portia's action—'she took a little razor, such as barbers occupy to pare men's nails, and, causing her maids and women to go out of her chamber, gave herself a great gash withal in her thigh, that she was straight all of a gore blood'—the historian proceeds to tell us that 'perceiving her husband was marvellously out of quiet, and that he would take no rest, even in her greatest pain of all she spake in this sort unto him. . . .' There follows a long speech which is the basis of Portia's words in Shakespeare's scene, after which 'With these words she shewed him her wound on her thigh, and told him what she had done to prove herself.' The graphic particularity of Plutarch's narrative makes it probable that young Gilburne was instructed to present a lurid spectacle of physical injury—a limping entry, evidence (as she kneels) of pain unobserved by her preoccupied husband, a final *coup de théâtre* as she raises her farthingale (or, in rising from her bed, has she braved 'the raw cold morning' in her night-gown?) and reveals her thigh 'all of a gore blood'.

(3) An interesting example of divergence from the source can be found in the episode, also from JULIUS CAESAR, of Cinna the Poet. In two separate accounts Plutarch states that the lynching of the harmless poet was the immediate *cause* of the conspirators' flight from the city:

'This made Brutus and his companions more afraid than any other thing, next unto the change of Antonius. Wherefore they got them out of Rome. . . .' In Shakespeare's play we are told that 'Brutus and Cassius Are rid like Madmen through the gates of Rome', *before* Cinna makes his luckless entry upon the Stage. The inference is that, while the news of the conspirators' flight keeps us abreast of the movement of the narrative, at this point of Shakespeare's design the death of the poet is more important, the culmination of the long first movement of the play—an ironical commentary on the effect of the noble Antony's oration, a no less ironical climax of the role of the Plebeians, transformed from the genial holiday-makers of the play's opening to the hysterical lynch-mob of its mid-way zenith. To drive the action relentlessly on to this point as to an inevitable climax is, as we can deduce from a study of the divergence from Plutarch, Shakespeare's architectural intention. The minor actors who have played the parts of the Commoners return in the later scenes of the play, doubling by necessity of numbers, and Shakespeare bestowed much care upon them (there is nothing perfunctory about the characterisation even of such briefly sketched figures as Pindarus, Volumnius and Strato); as the Commoners, led no doubt by the company's comedy gang, they would be apprised of the dramatic importance of their contribution to the whole structure of the play, and the gradual transition from good humour to berserk frenzy would be given due prominence in rehearsal: the phrase-by-phrase baiting of the poet, the whisper of his unlucky name running through the mob ('The first man told it to another, and that other unto another, so that it ran straight through them all . . .'), and the sudden explosion of irrational savagery ('Tear him for his bad verses. . . . Pluck but his name out of his heart . . .') would be no anti-climax after the virtuoso rabble-rousing of Antony's oration.

(4) Plutarch's accounts of this episode may also provide a clue to Shakespeare's intended characterisation. An unconsidered and perfunctory rendering of the poet Cinna's part might represent him as a figure of fun, a sort of helpless ass, the natural butt of men's mockery. But Plutarch's two versions of the story offer us (and offered Shakespeare) hints which suggest quite otherwise. In one, we are told that

'he was always one of Caesar's chiefest friends'; in the other, there is a plain inference that he left his house on that fateful day out of a sense of duty to his friend: '. . . hearing at that time that they burnt Caesar's body in the market-place, notwithstanding that he feared his dream, and had an ague on him besides, he came into the market-place to honour his funerals'. Poets in Queen Elizabeth's time were not, by definition, ridiculous: Shakespeare was a poet; Baldwin, in his cast-list for JULIUS CAESAR, even raises (with a question-mark) the possibility that the author played this little part himself. If so, Caesar's close friend may have resembled a Catullus, rather than a Bunthorne. Cinna does indeed, as Shakespeare draws him in brief sketch, behave like a poet. His opening words are sinister rather than absurd:

I dreamt tonight, that I did feast with Caesar . . .

The stress falls, with emphatic dismay, upon the word 'feast': to dine with a dead man is, as Plutarch makes clear, 'a marvellous strange and terrible dream'. Being a poet, the man is at the mercy of his imagination: '. . . things unluckily charge my Fantasy. . . .' Then, finding himself surrounded by a hostile and menacing rabble, he behaves with some presence of mind, with a brave defensive wit, and always like a poet; for it is the nature of poets to be critical of words, and it is the words of his aggressive questioners that he fastens on, repeating each of their questions, quizzing their provocative adverbs—'. . . to answer every man, directly and briefly, wisely and truly: wisely I say. . . .' When we remember Plutarch's account, there is dignity too, and some pathos, in his simple affirmation that he is going to Caesar's funeral 'as a friend'. He is dealing very sensibly and courageously with this unexpected and embarrassing encounter on his way to the ceremony; and it is just bad luck that his name is that of one of the conspirators. The victim of the lynch-mob's insensate rage is innocent, but (in the poet's portrait of a poet, modelled on Plutarch) he is no fool.

(5) Shakespeare was available to tell his fellow-actors what he meant: but we are not seldom confronted with a problem when the words he gave his actors to speak allow of more than one interpretation: the dramatic point of a whole episode may be ambiguous. In

such a case, a study of the source will sometimes provide a revealing clue. In the last scene of ANTONY AND CLEOPATRA there is such a dilemma. The Queen is now Caesar's prisoner, and, as proof of her submission, she offers him an inventory of all her possessions, claiming that she has reserved nothing for herself: she calls her steward Seleucus, to confirm the list. The steward will not 'speak that which is not', and when she asks 'What have I kept back?' he blandly answers:

Enough to purchase what you have made known.

Caesar bids Cleopatra 'blush not', and commends her wisdom in reserving some of her treasure for herself. But she flies into a violent rage against 'the ingratitude of this Seleucus', ending her tirade with a splendid display of indignation:

> Prithee go hence,
> Or I shall show the Cinders of my spirits
> Through th'Ashes of my chance . . .

Now it would be possible to play this scene at its face-value, the Egyptian Queen caught out in an ingenuous deception, humiliated in the presence of her Roman conqueror by the betrayal of a time-serving servant. But there is another, and subtler, interpretation (as Muir, 205, points out)—that Cleopatra is acting a part, because, though she is determined to take her own life, she wants (in order to achieve this purpose) to make Caesar believe that she means to continue living. This motive is quite clear in Plutarch's narrative, and especially in the marginal gloss: 'Cleopatra finely deceiveth Octavius Caesar, as though she desired to live.' No doubt Shakespeare (creator of Cleopatra's infinite variety) instructed his talented boy-actor to offer the audience a plain hint of the Queen's prepared collusion with her steward in the performance of this scene—an exchange of glances suggesting a code of conspiracy in her command 'Speak the truth Seleucus' and in her calculated prompting, 'What have I kept back?' This scene of stratagem plays its part in conveying to us that sense of a battle of wits which is the framework for the last Act of the play, with Caesar determined that Cleopatra shall live to grace his Roman triumph, and Cleopatra resolved to die. No sooner has Caesar left the stage, complacent after the revelations of Seleucus, than Cleopatra reminds us of that battle of wits:

> He words me Girls, he words me,
> That I should not be Noble to my self.

But the victory is hers, for she 'finely deceiveth' him, and the stratagem of the inventory gives a special force to her later jest, shared in confidence with the Asp, the pretty worm of Nilus, who is helping her to die:

> Oh could'st thou speak,
> That I might hear thee call great Caesar Ass,
> Unpolicied.

In deducing how Shakespeare's Cleopatra played this scene, Plutarch's evidence is a clue that must not be neglected.

(6) Browning, in *The Ring and the Book*, has occasion to speak of how

> a drudging student trims his lamp,
> Opens his Plutarch, puts him in the place
> Of Roman, Grecian . . .

At second remove, we may take pleasure in leaning over the shoulder of Shakespeare as he too opens his Plutarch. And if in the course of our conjecture the lamp seems sometimes in need of trimming (how ill this taper burns), there are moments when the wick is clean and the oil burns brightly, and we can glimpse the quick invention of this not so drudging student.

> Small have continual plodders ever won,
> Save base authority from others' Books . . .

But Shakespeare's way with a book was to devour it, we may guess, with his pen poised: his mind, they say, and hand went together. As, for instance, when he read in Plutarch's *Life of Coriolanus* about Martius's modest request from his commanding officer as a recompense for his heroism in battle: 'Among the Volsces there is an old friend and host of mine, an honest wealthy man, and now a prisoner, who living before in great wealth in his own country, liveth now a poor prisoner, in the hands of his enemies: and yet notwithstanding all this his misery and misfortune, it would do me great pleasure if I could save him from this one danger, to keep him from being sold as a slave.' Plutarch leaves us to assume that the request was granted; he says no more about the 'old friend and host', who is merely a symbol of Martius's 'great contentation and abstinence' in asking so little reward for his valour. Plutarch, the historian, does not even mention his name. And Shakespeare, the playwright, finds the historian's lofty insouciance amusing: his sense of humour is tickled by this anonymity, and he transfers Plutarch's casual omission to Martius himself. Cominius, his commander, commends the request:

> Oh well begg'd:
> Were he the butcher of my Son, he should
> Be free, as is the Wind: deliver him, Titus.

So Titus Lartius asks for the prisoner's name. And Shakespeare makes Burbage clap his hand to his brow in delightfully comic frustration:

> By Jupiter forgot:
> I am weary, yea, my memory is tir'd:
> Have we no wine here?

The poor man's fate is shelved: the hero has shown his magnanimity: isn't it time for a drink?

Such flashes of invention we may glimpse as the marks of opportunist genius. Sometimes the thought-process seems more gradual and more far-reaching. Early in Plutarch's *Life of Coriolanus* we are told that, when the common people forsook the city by way of protest against their ill-treatment by the rich, 'the Senate being afeard of their departure, did send unto them certain of the pleasantest old men, and the most acceptable to the people among them. Of those Menenius Agrippa was he, who was sent for chief man of the message from the Senate.' There follows, in bald outline, the 'notable tale' with which this Menenius 'knit up his oration in the end', the fable of the body's members revolting against the belly, which is told at such humorously patient length in the first scene of Shakespeare's play. That is the last we hear of Menenius in Plutarch's narrative. As is well known, from this small hint Shakespeare developed the richest personality-study in his play, and the character of Menenius Agrippa has a structural purpose in providing the right kind of dialectical opposition needed to draw out the unsubtle intransigence of the clamorous tribunes, and the right kind of warm commonsense to throw into relief the angry pride of Coriolanus. It may well be that Plutarch's phrase, 'the pleasantest old men', suggested these traits of personality to Shakespeare. Moreover, in the phrasing of Shakespeare's Menenius, we can hear echoes of a familiar style—to crack the wind of a poor phrase, a short tale to make, since brevity is the soul of wit—the reluctance to be hurried by impatient interruption; as when a too talkative, too assured citizen demands,

> What could the Belly answer?
> —I will tell you,
>   If you'll bestow a small (of what you have little)
>   Patience awhile; you'll hear the Belly's answer.
> —Y'are long about it.
> —Note me this good Friend;
>   Your most grave Belly was deliberate,
>   Not rash like his Accusers, and thus answered.

It is the style, the voice of Polonius, Egeus, Capulet, Brabantio, the familiar voice (as Baldwin so persuasively assigns it) of John Heminges. It is hard to resist the inference that, reading this brief paragraph of Plutarch, Shakespeare said 'Here is a part for Heminges', and began accordingly to elaborate it into the full-length portrait of the whimsical old patrician. Whether the genesis of the part was in Plutarch's phrase, or in Heminges's position in the company, or in a combination of the two, the part itself grew to such dimensions in its own right that it must be given its own development, its own individual existence, its own climax. The scene of Coriolanus's snubbing of his 'old Father Menenius' (wholly Shakespeare's invention) is based on a couple of sentences in Plutarch which do not mention Menenius: 'The ambassadors that were sent, were Martius' familiar friends and acquaintance, who looked at the least for a courteous welcome of him, as of their familiar friend and kinsman. Howbeit they found nothing less. . . .' Shakespeare's expansion—half-tragic, half-comic—of this episode has its affinities with the rejection of Falstaff, and, in the impersonation of Heminges, we may guess it did not lack a saving grace of absurdity: certainly there is pathos and a touch of dignity (Polonius had dignity too) in his departure after he has been so uncompromisingly put down: his withering scorn of the Watchmen's baiting has an undertone of inarticulate grief:

> I neither care for th'world, nor your General: for such things as you, I can scarce think there's any, y'are so slight. He that hath a will to die by himself, fears it not from another: Let your General do his worst. For you, be that you are, long; and your misery increase with your age. I say to you, as I was said to, Away.

But Heminges's echo of Burbage's sonorous 'Away' must have seemed like a pale parody. And if we are disposed to read too much of tragic sentiment into this episode, let us not forget that Shakespeare's Menenius does not die, but keeps the edge of his tongue sharp to give the trembling tribune Sicinius a deliberately exaggerated caricature of his fruitless visit to Coriolanus. There is, moreover, no suggestion of a broken heart or indeed of a blunted spirit, when the message comes that Rome is saved at the eleventh hour from destruction, by the embassy of Coriolanus's mother and wife. The irony of Volumnia's triumph, so mortal to her son, is not lost in the pleasant old man's contemptuous detachment. The jubilant music which welcomes the returning ladies is stressed both in the insistent stage-directions of the Folio, and in the eloquent detail of the Messenger's verbal description. There is surely a wry smile on old stuttering Heminges's face, as he stands apart from the penitently thankful tribune and his ecstatic informants, and listens to the general exultation in which his clear-sighted spirit has no part:

Hark, how they joy.

In these developments from a few sentences of Plutarch we see the strength and breadth of Shakespeare's dramatic invention.

(7) If we remember that Shakespeare was a poetic dramatist, that his chief means of creating drama was the spoken word of his actors, that as a poet he was especially sensitive to the power of the words he read, and that of all poets he was the most pictorial so that his own text is full of images created by verbal means, then we shall not be surprised to find that certain words, certain phrases, certain passages in his sources had a specially stimulating effect on his creative imagination. It is well known that Enobarbus's famous description of Cleopatra's first meeting with Antony is adapted in very close detail (and transformed by Shakespeare's own particular magic) from North's version of Plutarch; likewise that Prospero's no less famous valediction to his attendant spirits is indebted in close detail to Golding's translation of Ovid. To note these resemblances is to wonder at Shakespeare's opportunist skill in selecting from and adapting his material for an immediate dramatic purpose; to admire the genius which in each case so far transcends the original. But a close study of the sources can reveal more complex and abstruse trails in the detective quest which leads to a greater understanding of Shakespeare's craftsmanship as a poetic dramatist.

We beg the patience of our readers, to follow one such trail, again from Plutarch, in the hope that the source may help us to divine how Shakespeare's mind went to work on the central dilemma of JULIUS CAESAR. This may, in broad terms, be described as the question, how can a good man commit murder and remain good? Shakespeare has been at great pains to dramatise, in the spoken words of his soliloquies, the dilemma of 'poor Brutus with himself at war'; the problem appears not only in the direct exposition of soliloquy but also implicitly, in image and idea throughout the play. As Shakespeare reads his Plutarch, his sensitive ear, and his pictorial imagination, are arrested (we suggest) by one startling phrase—how Caesar 'was hackled and mangled among them, as a wild beast taken of hunters'. This is one aspect of the killing of Caesar, and it made a deep impression upon Shakespeare; for this striking image is clean contrary to any presentation of the act as the work of noble idealists. It is the image which occurs to Antony, of the 'Deer, strucken by many Princes', even when in the presence of Caesar's corpse he is pretending to compound with the assassins:

> here wast thou bay'd brave Hart,
> Here didst thou fall, and here thy Hunters stand
> Sign'd in thy Spoil, and Crimson'd in thy Lethe.

The same comparison may underlie Antony's later recollection of the moment of Caesar's death, when he taunts the murderers because they 'fawn'd like Hounds', and 'damned Casca, like a Cur, behind Struck Caesar on the neck'. But, very significantly, Shakespeare puts the image into Brutus's mouth too, at an earlier stage in the play, when he and his fellow-conspirators are discussing whether Antony should be killed as well as Caesar. No, says Brutus: 'Let's be Sacrificers, but not Butchers', and of Caesar's killing he adds:

> Let's carve him, as a Dish fit for the Gods,
> Not hew him as a Carcass fit for Hounds.

These are poetical images; all poetry is feigning; it were better, we might think, for Brutus if he based his actions on less slippery ground. Neither Antony's image of the hunt, nor Brutus's of sacrifice, can alter the stark fact of political assassination. And because he cannot resolve the dilemma in his soul, Brutus never ceases to be with himself at war until the moment of his own death. That the illusive idea of sacrifice is prominent in Brutus's thoughts (and was so in Shakespeare's conception), we can tell from that strange ceremony which Brutus initiates immediately after the killing of Caesar, the bathing of hands in Caesar's blood. The ceremony is not in Plutarch's account, and is Shakespeare's own invention. We cannot, of course, say with certainty that this cardinal contrast between two aspects of Caesar's death (butchery and sacrifice) arose in Shakespeare's mind from one phrase of Plutarch's—'a wild beast taken of hunters'. But this speculation, and other such, are worth making if we want to guess how Shakespeare's fellows in rehearsal developed his written intention. Burbage's emphasis upon sacrifice as he talked with his confederates in the garden at night, and as he knelt beside the bleeding body of his victim, Condell's upon the blooding of the hunters, are key-notes in the poet's overall design, if we have read Shakespeare's reading of Plutarch aright. Certainly, as we let imagination dwell upon those mornings of rehearsal in the playhouse, any hint, any clue, that can help us to overhear the conversation between Shakespeare and his fellow-actors is to the purpose. The foremost topic, we may be sure, of such conversation was the means of giving most potent dramatic effect to the words which the poet supplied for his actors to speak.

THE ACTOR'S TASK

From the study, then, of the structure and circumstance of Shakespeare's playhouse, of the company of players to which he belonged and their acting style, of the visual aspect of his stage in terms of costume, properties and furniture, and of the audible accompaniment of music and sound-effects, from the study too of the transmission of his written material, and of the sources of his inspiration—from all these studies, which lead towards a closer understanding of the processes of Shakespeare's craftsmanship, one fundamental truth emerges with unmistakable clarity. Shakespeare's playhouse bred a poetic drama; his use of all his theatrical resources was eminently skilful, but they were only subordinate aids to his most potent art; it was the spoken word, supported by the miming and posture and gesture of the speakers, which in the presence of those heterogeneous and diversely critical audiences created the illusion of his imagined living world.

And the quality of Shakespeare's spoken word compels us to assume that his colleagues were highly skilled speakers—from Richard Burbage himself down to the young apprentices for whom it was worth writing the subtleties of Rosalind and Beatrice and Belmont's Portia. Their skill had the professional calibre that belongs in our day to the operatic singer, requiring as much training and practice and musicianship as is expected of him. This must have been so, because of the playhouse conditions, where speech was the chief medium of appeal. But the converse too of this proposition needs stating: that it is only when we think of the words of Shakespeare's text as being spoken in the conditions of his playhouse, that we can appreciate the skill of his players, and by an obvious corollary the detailed perfection of the playwright. He was, unlike most of his contemporary dramatists, an actor, constantly engaged in the process of staging and rehearsal, and he learnt in play after play to improve and expand the expressive power of his medium. The evidence survives in the early printed texts: and a systematic exploration of Shakespeare's craftsmanship in terms of the playhouse for which he made his plays is long overdue. A necessary prelude to such a comprehensive and detailed examination is to consider what kind of expertise the poet could expect—and plainly did expect—from his fellow-players in the interpretation of his text. By studying the elements of their technique we may come to realise some at least of the functions of the spoken word in giving substance to the Poet's Method.

*　　*　　*

To understand and communicate the **Sense** was their first task. We may assume that Shakespeare's fellows avoided the obvious blunders caused by simple misunderstanding: with him at their elbow they would not have been able to misinterpret those famous phrases whose ambiguity of syntax or sense still puzzles the schoolboy—Macbeth's 'Making the Green one Red', for instance, or Hamlet's 'a Custom More honour'd in the breach, than the observance'. They would have known how often the audience's grasp of the narrative issues of a play depended upon the clear communication of verbal sense; for in this theatre, where the spoken word is the dramatist's chief instrument, essential preliminaries of narrative and situation are not seldom conveyed in the dialogue— just as in the cinema the technique of flash-back action may clarify the story. Not only emotion but also perfect precision of meaning must be conveyed in Iago's bitter account of his thwarted hopes of promotion, in Prospero's resentful narrative of his usurping brother's perfidy, and in the Duke of Vienna's temperate description of poor Mariana's betrayal by the well-seeming Angelo. It is not enough to speak, but to speak true. This may seem obvious: yet it is no uncommon experience, when listening to a play of Shakespeare, that we wake up to realise that we have not understood a word of what the actor has been saying. That hypnotic verse-speaking voice, taking no risk of decisive emphasis, leaves us entranced perhaps, but not illuminated. Shakespeare, one may guess, who liked it trippingly on the tongue, would have had none of this; and the problem is not only one of the clear exposition of narrative. If the boy Goffe tried to intone 'The quality of mercy . . .' as if it had already been hallowed in a hundred eclectic anthologies, he would have been brusquely bidden to come off his fence of bogus dignity and consider what the words (in their context) mean. Faced by a seemingly insoluble dilemma of law, Portia, so wisely youthful in her lawyer's robes, has pointed out the obvious solution of humanity:

Then must the Jew be merciful.

Shylock's reply is a calculated sneer:

On what compulsion must I? Tell me that.

In Goffe's performance, her retort is indignant, impulsive and warm-hearted:

The quality of mercy

(the very essence of it)

is not strain'd,

(is not a matter of compulsion)

It droppeth as the gentle rain from heaven
Upon the place beneath.

Similarly, a careful consideration of the dramatic context will help to clarify the problem of sense which arises at that moment of intense climax in the last Act of MACBETH, when the beleaguered tyrant is told of the death of his wife, her whom he once called 'My dearest Partner of Greatness':

The Queen (my Lord) is dead.

In the brief pause which follows these pregnant words, we must be wondering what Macbeth's reaction will be: it may surprise us, it may disappoint us, it may touch us, it may horrify us. In Burbage's response (whatever may have been its emotional ambiguity) the syntactical relation which communicates sense would have been plain enough:

> She should have di'd hereafter;
> There would have been a time for such a word...

There is in the 'hereafter': a brief pressure of emphasis on the word makes this point of meaning clear. Burbage had the advantage over us, for the author himself was there to tell him what he meant. We may be sure that he was explicit, and did not play for safety (as many of your Players do) in a dignified but self-defeating obscurity. Shakespeare too would have told Heminges that at the moment of Lear's death, when Kent murmurs 'Break heart, I prithee break', it is his master's heart he speaks of, not his own; and would have begged the actor to cry 'Vex not his ghost' with a kind of indignant rebuke to Edgar's youthful hope of penultimate revival.

Often, then, the meaning will depend upon a simple and decisive planting of *Emphasis*. The emphasis however may be elaborate and its distribution complicated. King Henry the Fourth's rating of his unsatisfactory son, Prince Hal, is an extended exercise in the distribution of logical and contrasting emphases. Hal, it seems, is taking the same road to ruin as his father's predecessor, King Richard the Second (the 'skipping King', as Henry calls him). Typical of Henry's didactic distinctions is one of the several images in which he remembers Richard's fault of being too free with his society:

> So when he had occasion to be seen,
> He was but as the Cuckoo is in June,
> Heard, not regarded.

Only by emphasis of voice can Shakespeare's meaning be conveyed: Richard was not just like a cuckoo, but like a cuckoo in *June* (by which month in England the welcome visitor of spring has become wearisome): and emphasis of voice is needed again to point the antithesis: in June he is *heard* as much as ever, but nobody *regards* him.

The communication of sense sometimes obliges the player to make the audience aware of the *Irony* underlying his words. Among several phrases of double-entendre in the speech of King Henry the Fifth, as he plays cat-and-mouse with the three men who have conspired against his life on the quay-side at Southampton, there is one peculiarly sinister: he asks them whether they do not think his army will be sufficient to win victory over the French, and Scroop (whom he has thought to be his bosom-friend) answers:

> No doubt my Liege, if each man do his best.

This is the King's reply:

> I doubt not that, since we are well persuaded
> We carry not a heart with us from hence,
> That grows not in a fair consent with ours:
> Nor leave not one behind, that doth not wish
> Success and Conquest to attend on us.

The point Burbage is asked to make here is that the King has no intention of taking the three traitors with him to France, nor does he purpose to leave them behind: he speaks the words in such a way that his audience understand the ironical point, but the traitors may take them at their face-value—a nice calculation (nicely recognised in the Folio's colon and subsequent comma) of hesitation and emphasis. Deliberate irony is so pervasive in the plays of Shakespeare that he clearly took its use for granted as part of the equipment of his fellow-players. It is ingrained in the very personality of Hamlet, but it appears also in the passing phrases of minor characters such as the Scottish Doctor who, when Macbeth, roaring his defiance of the approaching English, asks 'Hear'st thou of them?', drily answers:

> Ay my good Lord: your Royal Preparation
> Makes us hear something.

Shakespeare demanded the skilful use of this weapon even from his apprentice-players. The familiar boy-girl disguise of the comedies provides frequent opportunities. Rosalind, masquerading as a young man, lectures her unwitting suitor Orlando on the jealousies and tantrums of women after they are married, and pretending for the moment to be Orlando's wife, paints a horrifying picture of post-honeymoon matrimony:

> I will be more jealous of thee, than a Barbary cock-pigeon over his hen, more clamorous than a Parrot against rain . . . I will weep for nothing . . . I will laugh like a Hyen, and that when thou art inclin'd to sleep.

Orlando, disturbed by the daunting prospect she describes, asks, 'But will my Rosalind do so?' And 'By my life, she will do' (answers the disguised Rosalind) 'as I do.' What would we not give to hear the boy-player being rehearsed in the morning in the utterance of that little sentence of nine words? He must be taught to solve the familiar problem of deliberate irony, that delicate balance of tone by which the audience becomes aware not only of the double meaning but also of the speaker's awareness of it, while the other characters on the stage seem plausibly to be unaware.

Shakespeare also expected the players to give due point to his *Word-Play*. Deliberate punning word-play has become fashionable again among the writers of the twentieth century, and its continuing popularity as a staple feature of comic entertainment encourages the belief that this familiar weapon in the poet's armoury is by no means obsolete today. Shakespeare uses it constantly, and for a variety of purposes, by no means only comic. It is especially characteristic of his earlier plays, as in the adolescent gusto of this line of exuberant vituperation:

> For Suffolk's Duke, may he be suffocate . . .

Richard of Gloucester shows a subtler wit in his exercise of an ambiguous paradox: speaking to his brother Clarence, he drily complains of Queen Elizabeth's dominant influence in the court:

> We are the Queen's abjects, and must obey.

Burbage will leave us in no doubt that his nimble tongue has veered aside from the conventional formula of 'the Queen's subjects'. Wordplay pervades the text of ROMEO AND JULIET. Mercutio, baiting Romeo's melancholy, says:

> You are a Lover, borrow Cupid's wings,
> And soar with them above a common bound.

To which Romeo answers:

> I am too sore enpierced with his shaft,
> To soar with his light feathers, and so bound,
> I cannot bound a pitch above dull woe . . .

The young bloods of Verona may become tiresome with their self-conscious quibbles: but out of this same punning trick is forged this sentence of Mercutio dying; Mercutio, whose high spirits have illuminated the play hitherto, dies with a jest on his lips:

> Ask for me tomorrow, and you shall find me a grave man.

His word-play, for all its tragic import, may draw (since it is uttered by a habitual jester) a tribute of rueful laughter from the sympathetic audience. But no such laughter is evoked by Lady Macbeth's grim quibble, as she carries the blood-stained daggers back into the chamber of death:

> I'll gild the Faces of the Grooms withal,
> For it must seem their Guilt.

Yet we may be sure that young John Edmans was not allowed to slur over the relation between the words 'gild' and 'guilt'. Nor would Burbage allow us to miss Hamlet's characteristic ambiguity in the very first words of this long and most exacting of parts. When King Claudius says to him, in a tone which combines coaxing with complacent patronage,

But now my Cousin Hamlet, and my Son . . .

Hamlet mutters aside,

A little more than kin, and less than kind.

Then to the King's question,

How is it that the Clouds still hang on you?

he flashes out:

Not so my Lord, I am too much i'th'Sun.

On the printed page we are forced to settle for one spelling or the other of two like-sounding words. The ear of the audience makes no such selection. Too much in the *sun*? Not therefore overcast with clouds; he is a lone figure, dressed in rebellious black, enduring the sunlit splendour of the marriage-guests at court. Too much in the *son*? This, then, is an angry rejection of Claudius's usurping paternal address. To bring the double point of this ambiguity home to the audience, requires no doubt the use of eye and posture as well as voice: but all Burbage's experienced skill will be directed to making us uncomfortably aware of the two meanings of that comprehensive monosyllable.

That a sufficient majority of Shakespeare's audience were attuned to appreciate verbal subtlety is plain from the frequency with which *Contests of Wit* abound in the earlier plays of the canon. LOVE'S LABOUR'S LOST is almost built of them, with the sets of wit well played between the mocking wenches of the French court and the

King's little Academe of fellow-scholars. Less formal but no less brilliant are the bouts of raillery between Beatrice and Benedick, and Feste's fencing with Viola and with Orsino, Prince Hal's teasing of Falstaff, and Hamlet's of Polonius. In the continuously expanding scope of Shakespeare's art these contests of wit (based on a foundation of elementary word-play) became more and more closely integrated into the dramatic unity of the plays. We may be sure that, accustomed thus to quick-fire and complex repartee, Shakespeare's audiences responded immediately to the close verbal texture of the later plays; as when to Lear's angry command, 'Out of my sight', Kent's riposte is both swift and apt:

> See better Lear, and let me still remain
> The true blank of thine eye.

The wrangling of Antony and Cleopatra, no less than the villains' empty-hearted mockery of old Gonzalo, depended upon the nimble tongues of the players and the keen ears of the audience.

Interpreters of Shakespeare today—whether actors, directors or students—have one problem which his contemporaries were spared; Shakespeare's coinages, fire-new from the mint of his imagination, have become hackneyed by repeated quotation. It is the penalty of their aptness. Why, it has been asked, did Shakespeare put so many quotations into HAMLET? It is not surprising that, when so many of his phrases have passed into the common usage, we fall into the way of taking for clichés what are in fact exact and precise and pointed expressions. All too often, in fact, the reason for an unintelligent and unintelligible delivery of Shakespeare's lines is an unconscious underrating of his poetic skill. The cliché may conceal a vigorous metaphor. Achilles, when he hears that Ajax, rather than he, is to have the honour of single combat with Hector, says:

> I see my reputation is at stake . . .

The sentence sounds prosaic, until he continues:

My fame is shrewdly gored.

Then we see that his reputaion is compared to a bear in the neighbour-ing bear-pit chained to a stake, and gored by the baiting dogs. Shakes-peare's actor perhaps reinforced this metaphor with an illustrative posture of martyrdom. Again, it is all too easy to overlook (in the familiar formula of 'one fell swoop') the terrifying image embodied in Macduff's anguish as he hears that his family has been annihilated:

> All my pretty ones?
> Did you say All? Oh Hell-Kite! All?
> What, All my pretty Chickens, and their Dam
> At one fell swoop?

On the Globe Stage we should be made to see (with the mind's eye) the single murderous dive with which the bird of prey devastates the whole defenceless farm-yard. Sometimes indeed in familiar usage a phrase has changed its meaning. When Othello demands proof that his wife is unfaithful, Iago offers his repulsive story of Cassio's adul-terous dream; in the face of Othello's agony, he blandly observes that dreams are not to be interpreted as reality, but for his tortured victim suspicion has become certainty: the dream, he cries, 'denoted a fore-gone conclusion'. In the context of Shakespeare's play, a foregone conclusion is not, in the sense of the modern catch-phrase, a pre-determined future result, but (as the Folio's hyphen helps to remind us) the real and previous experience of which the dream was an imaginative re-enactment. Always Shakespeare's fellow-actors would be on their guard against a slovenly and perfunctory interpretation. Macbeth speaks enviously about the dead King Duncan, whom he has murdered for his crown:

> After Life's fitful Fever, he sleeps well . . .

'Life's fitful Fever' sounds hackneyed enough. But a few days in bed with a high temperature will restore the bright surface of this metaphor. To Shakespeare's audiences a 'fit' is a crisis of fever: this word is part of the pervasive imagery of the play. When later Macbeth discovers that Fleance has escaped his murderous intent, he feels again a sense of crisis: 'Then comes my Fit again.' 'Fitful' was Shakespeare's own coinage, and its sense was precise. In the crisis of fever you can get no rest; and then, blessedly, comes the relief as the fever leaves you; then (like Duncan) you sleep well. Macbeth—poor man—as he speaks, cannot get any rest.

*   *   *

If we consider what further kind of instruction the seasoned members of the company gave to their boy-apprentices, certainly high among the priorities, after the communication of the Sense, would have been a study of the **Shape** of the poet's text and practice in the rendering of his ingeniously varied phrasing. Patterns of speech and writing were a commonplace of the time. Both verse and prose (and not only in the playhouse) depended for much of their effect upon the use of verbal patterns; and the ears of the audience, attuned to the measured periods and balanced antitheses of Cranmer's Prayer Book, would be ready to appreciate new variations of shape at the prompting of the poet and through the expert diction of his interpreters.

A simple example of such phrasing can be found in four lines of THE RAPE OF LUCRECE:

> The patient dies while the physician sleeps;
> The orphan pines while the oppressor feeds . . .

Here we have exact correspondence; the two statements are balanced word for word: *patient—orphan*: *dies—pines*: *physician—oppressor*: *sleeps —feeds*. Now mark the inversion: as the poet continues in the next two lines to make parallel statements, he expresses them in an opposite order:

> Justice is feasting while the widow weeps . . .

Here *justice* in this line plays the part of *the physician* and *the oppressor* in the previous lines: *the widow* is the equivalent of *the patient* and *the orphan*. The fourth line repeats the inverted order of the third. If the reader will speak aloud the whole passage, he will hear the change of order which Shakespeare intends him to hear:

> The patient dies while the physician sleeps;
> The orphan pines while the oppressor feeds;
> Justice is feasting while the widow weeps;
> Advice is sporting while infection breeds.

Without this inversion of the pattern, the passage loses its shape, and together with its shape its epigrammatic force.

Balance is the basis of much of the impassioned rhetoric of the first cycle of English histories. A most striking example occurs in RICHARD III. There are three women on the Stage, all in mourning: the old Queen Margaret, widow of Henry the Sixth, is crowing at long last over the downfall of her supplanter, Queen Elizabeth, who is now widow of Edward the Fourth:

> If sorrow can admit society,
> Tell over your woes again by viewing mine,
> I had an Edward, till a Richard kill'd him:
> I had a Harry, till a Richard kill'd him:
> Thou hadst an Edward, till a Richard kill'd him:
> Thou hadst a Richard, till a Richard kill'd him.

The monotony of the repeated phrase is deliberate, and the boy-player is taught not to be afraid of giving it its full force; but a variation of emphasis gives new interest to the second repetition ('*Thou* hadst an Edward . . .'), and at the third repetition a still different emphasis ('Thou hadst a *Richard* . . .') makes a new pattern with the already familiar, almost hackneyed, phrase. This killer Queen Margaret speaks of is, of course, Richard the Crookback; and it is this Richard's mother, the Duchess of York, who interrupts her:

> I had a Richard too, and thou didst kill him;
> I had a Rutland too, thou holpst to kill him.

131

And Queen Margaret rounds on her, in gathering passion:

> Thou hadst a Clarence too, and Richard kill'd him.
> From forth the kennel of thy womb hath crept
> A Hell-hound that doth hunt us all to death.

Each one of these violent deaths has been enacted on the Stage, or reported in narration, in the course of Shakespeare's historical cycle; so each has its special impact on the sympathies or antipathies of the audience. There is no danger of the poet's method seeming absurd, as if his catalogue has run to seed in a sort of conundrum. On the contrary, the climax is overwhelming, and the climax is made possible by the repetitive balance.

The same play has a poignant example, where the patterned balance is combined with word-play, so that both sense and shape are involved. Richard Crookback is upbraiding his brother's widow, Queen Elizabeth, for thwarting him in his plans, and he says, snappishly:

> Your Reasons are too shallow, and too quick.

Her answer is shrewdly prompt:

> O no, my Reasons are too deep and dead,
> Too deep and dead (poor Infants) in their graves . . .

'Deep' is her retort to 'shallow'; 'dead' to 'quick'. She makes a pattern to match his phrase, and with the pattern she combines a deliberate and pathetic distortion of sense. Her children were the little princes, smothered in the Tower of London by Richard's command. To give due force to such a passage was expected as a matter of routine from the boy-apprentices of the Chamberlain's company.

This balanced speech has its comic equivalent, as may be heard in an intricate flourish of Berowne's, protesting against his royal master's insistence (in face of the unexpected visit of the French Princess and her ladies) on their keeping intact their vow of monastic celibacy. It is to be expected of Berowne that there will be much wit in the variations of his pattern:

For Wisdom's sake, a word that all men love:
Or for Love's sake, a word that loves all men.
Or for Men's sake, the author of these Women:
Or Women's sake, by whom we men are Men.
Let's once lose our oaths to find our selves,
Or else we lose our selves, to keep our oaths . . .

Both a discriminating intellect and an agile tongue are needed in the
actor who is to understand and communicate the extremely complex
scheme of these lines, in which the key words—wisdom, love, men,
women, lose, find, keep, oaths, selves—chime against each other in a
constantly and rapidly varying ringer's change.

Habitual practice and delivery of such patterned phrasing taught
Shakespeare's fellows that feeling of all kinds, even tragic, could be
communicated on their Stage in deliberately formal speech. Of such a
kind is the measured pathos of Richard the Second's resignation. It
may have been Burbage's habit to point this passage with contrasted
pairs of gestures; for his task was to bring each image and its opposite before the mind's eye of the audience; but it is unlikely that he
would have allowed the King's grief to disrupt the verbal scheme—
indeed, in this particular case, the surface self-consciousness is part of
the dramatic effect which the poet is seeking to make:

I'll give my Jewels for a set of Beads,
My gorgeous Palace, for a Hermitage,
My gay Apparel, for an Alms-man's Gown,
My figur'd Goblets, for a Dish of Wood,
My Sceptre, for a Palmer's walking Staff,
My Subjects, for a pair of carved Saints,
And my large Kingdom, for a little Grave,
A little little Grave, an obscure Grave.

The Folio's commas and capital letters give an accurate record of
the pattern. This kind of balanced catalogue is not confined to verse
forms. Often it gives rhythmic life to a prose climax. So Thomas
Pope makes us hear the incantation which underlies Shylock's mount-

ing anger—four moods embodied in succession through the varied
tone-colour of his versatile tongue:

> If you prick us do we not bleed? if you tickle us, do we not
> laugh? if you poison us do we not die? and if you wrong us shall
> we not revenge?

The pattern sometimes involves more than one speaker. No less
formal than Richard's elegy, and sometimes as full of feeling, are the
frequent instances of antiphonal poetry, as between Lorenzo and
Jessica, or Hermia and Helena; there is an air of public performance in
the four lines of stichomythia which first introduce us to Antony and
Cleopatra; more intricate in pattern, and self-conscious in the different
sense of youthful shyness, is the divided sonnet in which Romeo and
Juliet first speak to each other. But patterns of speech are not incompatible with sudden spontaneity of feeling: the stock-punished Kent's
resolute and humorous response to his master's indignant inquisition
gains greatly by the precision of verbal echo:

> —What's he, that hath so much thy place mistook
>   To set thee here?
> —It is both he and she,
>   Your Son, and Daughter.
> —No.
> —Yes.
> —No I say.
> —I say yea.

(The chiasmus is a deliberate and effective variation)

> —No no, they would not.
> —Yes they have.
> —By Jupiter I swear no.
> —By Juno, I swear ay.

The device of formal speech-patterns is not reserved only for exceptional cases, for climaxes comic or lyrical or tragic, but is a habitual mode of the poet's expression, even when he had come to develop a freer and more spontaneous style: throughout the plays single patterned phrases sharply point an emphasis or clinch a cadence or convey a feeling with aphoristic precision.

The proper pointing of *Antithesis* is another accomplishment which the poet could expect from his actors. It is easy, on the printed page, for a reader to overlook the simple contrast as King Richard the Second commends the bringer of bad news:

> Too well, too well thou tell'st a Tale so ill.

But the actor will apply enough emphasis, within the dynamic range of the whole sentence, to the word 'ill', so as to make the poet's point clear. Much practice is demanded of the boy who plays Helena, if he is to do justice to the poor girl's frantic protest, when her scornful lover Demetrius means to leave her to the mercy of wild beasts in the Athenian wood:

> The wildest hath not such a heart as you;
> Run when you will, the story shall be chang'd:
> Apollo flies, and Daphne holds the chase;
> The Dove pursues the Griffin, the mild Hind
> Makes speed to catch the Tiger. Bootless speed,
> When cowardice pursues, and valour flies.

For the audience must be made aware that for Apollo to fly is a paradox, that in the normal course of things doves do not pursue griffins, nor hinds go out of their way to hunt tigers. If the serial antithesis of this passage is not conveyed by a studied contrast of pitch in the speaker's voice, the poet's intended effect is lost upon the unprompted ear of the hearer. Sometimes, as we might expect, the poet uses antitheses (like his other verbal devices) as an instrument for revealing character or dramatic situation. Our first impression of King Claudius is of glib diplomacy registered in the nice calculation of antithesis; the gulf between the reality of political assassination and Brutus's idealised and honourable vision is subtly communicated in a long speech ('Our course will seem too bloody . . .') which is an extended exercise in the use of antithesis.

Shakespeare's demands on his players in reproducing the shape of his text are formidable indeed, and cannot have been met except by the most detailed training and assiduous practice, the sort of discipline which is exemplified in the exercises, scales, arpeggios and technical studies of the professional musician. Consider, for instance, Puck's tour-de-force, as he routs the mechanicals, upon Bottom's appearance from the hawthorn-brake, translated with the Ass-head on his shoulders:

> I'll follow you, I'll lead you about a Round,
> Through bog, through bush, through brake, through briar,
> Sometime a horse I'll be, sometime a hound:
> A hog, a headless bear, sometime a fire,
> And neigh, and bark, and grunt, and roar, and burn,
> Like horse, hound, hog, bear, fire, at every turn.

The last couplet of this highly organised six-line stanza requires the boy first to make five different imitative sounds, and then to echo them in quick succession. It demands diligent practice, but Shakespeare's coloratura Puck will have made it plain that it is the horse that neighs, the hound barks, the hog grunts, the bear (even without his head) roars, and the fire burns. Ophelia has a less breath-taking task of verbal association with the line,

> The Courtier's, Soldier's, Scholar's: Eye, tongue, sword . . .

but Enobarbus's deliberately extravagant mockery of the device exceeds both in organised diversity:

> . . . hearts, tongues, figures, scribes, bards, poets, cannot
> Think, speak, cast, write, sing, number—hoo!—
> His love to Antony.

Iterance (Shakespeare's own word for the deliberate and insistent repetition of a word or phrase) is a powerful device for increasing dramatic momentum and cementing continuity. Othello tries to justify the murder of his wife to the shocked Emilia by citing the evidence of Iago: 'Ask thy husband else.' First Emilia's incredulity and then her growing awareness of Iago's treachery are expressed in the insistent repetition of 'Husband' which provides the framework for the ensuing dialogue, until Othello bursts out:

> What needs this iterance, Woman? . . .
> I say thy Husband: dost understand the word?
> My Friend, thy Husband; honest, honest Iago.

Most powerfully horrible is the third-degree examination of poor Gloucester, when Regan and her husband Cornwall demand where he has sent old King Lear to save him from their clutches:

> *Reg.* Wherefore to Dover? Wast thou not charg'd at peril . . .
> *Corn.* Wherefore to Dover? Let him answer that.
> *Glos.* I am tied to th'Stake, and I must stand the Course.
> *Reg.* Wherefore to Dover?

Shylock's relentless 'I will have my bond', and Antony's 'Honourable man', used most skilfully with an effect of cumulative irony, are other examples of this phenomenon of iterance; and, in a lighter vein, Francis Flute's 'sixpence a day': it is a favourite device of Shakespeare's, and is used for a great variety of purposes.

Another means by which he gives life and continuity to his dialogue is the habit of making one speaker *pick up* the words of another. Two passages we have quoted for other reasons offer examples of this technique. The irony of Henry the Fifth's answer to Scroop is increased by a deliberately pointed echo:

> No doubt my Liege, if each man do his best.
> —I *doubt* not that . . .

Similarly Shylock's sneer is conveyed in a mocking echo:

> Then must the Jew be merciful.
> —On what compulsion *must* I?

Only the slipshod player will omit the small pointing of emphasis which knits the continuity of the dialogue. An extension of this technique is the practice of making one speaker pick up and *reinterpret* the words of another. Richard the Second's Queen tries to rally her fallen lord with the words

> wilt thou, Pupil-like,
> Take thy Correction mildly, kiss the Rod,
> And fawn on Rage with base Humility,
> Which art a Lion and a King of Beasts?

and he replies:

> A King of Beasts indeed: if aught but Beasts,
> I had been still a happy King of Men.

The shifting of the emphasis from 'King' to 'Beasts' makes the point: the words are the same, but their sense has changed: it is a poetical device by which the Queen's rallying phrase is shown to have another, less comfortable, meaning. A subtle example of this reinterpretation can be heard in HAMLET. 'Oh day and night' says Horatio of Hamlet's behaviour after he has seen the Ghost: 'but this is wondrous strange.' And Hamlet's reply (thinking of the poor Ghost, his father) is this:

> And therefore as a stranger give it welcome.

It is what you should do to strangers—welcome them. But Hamlet's word 'stranger' is bred out of Horatio's word 'strange', and the point is made with the inflection of Burbage's voice. To ignore and neglect the pattern involved in such repetitions of word and phrase is like playing music with no regard for marks of expression or phrasing. It was part of the equipment of the Shakespearian company to feel and reproduce the Shape of the poet's text, as well as its Sense.

* * *

They would moreover be at pains to study and communicate his acutely subtle (and in the course of the canon continually developing) manipulation of **Sound**. As we have already hinted, there is far more evidence of Shakespeare's intentions in the seemingly accidental irregularities of the early printed texts than has been usually supposed. No doubt there was established in the ear of every member of the company the regular iambic stress of the pentameter line, and the common variations and less common distortions of it. They would know—or Shakespeare would have told them—that (as with the barlines and time-signatures of music) you cannot vary unless you feel the underlying norm. They would by habit feel the end of the line and make their audience feel it too. Here is a normal and typical pentameter passage from JULIUS CAESAR:

> I cannot tell, what you and other men
> Think of this life: But for my single self,
> I had as lief not be, as live to be
> In awe of such a Thing, as I my self.
> I was born free as Caesar, so were you,
> We both have fed as well, and we can both
> Endure the Winter's cold, as well as he.

Phillips as Cassius marks the ends of these lines, not with an unnatural pause, but with just enough holding up of the flowing rhythm, or with variation in the voice of pitch, volume or emphasis, to indicate the lineation. The passage contains an interesting point of detail: there is a pattern of phrasing in the balance of the words 'as lief not be' and 'as live to be'; it is almost word-play, it is certainly balance; the poet's effect is lost if no mark is made of the end of the line. In a misguided pursuit of what is loosely called realism, some actors will lean over backwards to disguise from their audience where the line ends, and hurry naturalistically over the second 'be' on to an emphatic 'awe'.

But Shakespeare's pattern demands a momentary suspension after the second parallel of this verbal equipoise.

The players would be used to study and practise those deliberate short lines and defective lines which Alexander Pope, for instance, in his edition of Shakespeare was at such pains to smooth out into regularity. Flatter, in *Shakespeare's Producing Hand*, draws attention to many such lines where the incompleteness of the line's rhythm—the metrical gaps, as he calls them—have dramatic force. He quotes Lady Macbeth's

> The Raven himself is hoarse,
> That croaks the fatal entrance of Duncan
> Under my Battlements. Come you Spirits,
> That tend on mortal thoughts, unsex me here . . .

and adds 'Whether the actress takes a step forward, or raises her arms, or looks round, or simply takes a deep breath: there will always be a small pause; the text itself demands it imperatively—and here the pause is, clearly shown by the gap in the metre: between "battlements" and "Come" one syllable is missing.' Flatter mentions, with proper disapproval, the patching of the editors—Pope's 'Come, all you spirits', Steevens's 'Come, come, you spirits', and even in a modern edition the suggestion of 'Come, you ill spirits'. 'One wonders'—this is his final comment—'whether Shakespeare would be grateful for such collaboration.'[25] His own collaborators would be encouraged to accept, and communicate, his deliberate disturbance of the normal regularity of pentameter rhythm.

It need hardly be said that the early printed texts are not always helpful in this matter: the Folio ignores, and the Quarto only partially recognises, the striking combination of regular and short lines in Horatio's address to the Ghost of old Hamlet. Nevertheless Condell's Horatio would mark the expectant silences of his appeal to this unresponsive apparition:

> If thou hast any sound, or use of Voice,
> Speak to me.
> If there be any good thing to be done,

That may to thee do ease, and grace to me,
Speak to me.
If thou art privy to thy Country's Fate
(Which happily foreknowing may avoid)
Oh speak.

The actor would make us hear the iambic clock ticking in the empty
lines, like Horatio's heart-beat, waiting for the answer that does not
come.

Assonance is another of Shakespeare's habits, by which he gives his
verse a richer texture. Henry the Fifth proclaims

I will not leave the half-achieved Harfleur . . .

King Duncan praises Macbeth to his fellow-general:

True, worthy Banquo: he is full so valiant,
And in his commendations, I am fed:
It is a Banquet to me.

Mark Antony, when he hears news of Cleopatra's death, expresses his
despair in a most moving assonance:

All length is Torture: since the Torch is out,
Lie down and stray no further.

When Regan greets her father with a perfunctory welcome,

I am glad to see your Highness . . .

Lear's quick retort is this:

Regan, I think you are. I know what reason
I have to think so . . .

The exact degree of emphasis to be given to these musical echoes is a matter of taste and discretion: but certainly the King's Men did not ignore or disregard them. The hearer may not be conscious of the poet's effect; but the echo plays upon his ear and teases it with a beguiling impression. This would not happen unless the actor knew what the poet was doing, and turned his tongue to make the point. How often at morning rehearsal must Shakespeare have spent time and patience in ensuring the detailed realisation of his musical score.

The conscious use of sound for *Imitation* or *Evocation* would also need practice. There are effects of simple onomatopoeia, as when the mad Lear imagines the flight of an arrow:

> O well flown Bird: i'th'clout, i'th'clout: Hewgh.

More subtly, by evocation rather than imitation, Prospero recalls in the sound of his words that storm in which he and his infant daughter were set adrift by his enemies:

> There they hoist us
> To cry to th'Sea, that roar'd to us; to sigh
> To th'winds, whose pity sighing back again
> Did us but loving wrong . . .

More subtle still is the conjuring up of mood and feeling in sound, passages where (in Pope's phrase) 'the sound must seem an echo of the sense':

> 'Tis not alone my Inky Cloak (good Mother)
> Nor Customary suits of solemn Black . . .

Burbage consciously produces, so that his audience may unconsciously feel, the effect of Hamlet's disgust in the sounds of 'k' and 's'—an effect more clearly audible still in the spitting sibilants of his later soliloquy:

> O most wicked speed, to post
> With such dexterity to Incestuous sheets.

So too the very sound of the words marks the dramatic contrast between Lear's defiance of the storm,

> thou all-shaking Thunder,
> Strike flat the thick Rotundity o'th'world,
> Crack Nature's moulds . . .

and the helpless simplicity (but, with the cunning deception of concealed art, wrapped in the child-like rocking rhythm of a nursery-rhyme) of his realisation that his wits begin to turn:

> Come on my boy. How dost my boy? Art cold?
> I am cold my self.

Every reader of Shakespeare will have his favourite instance of the poet's manipulation of sound—the tripping rhythm of the Fairy's 'Over hill, over dale, thorough bush, thorough briar . . .'; the brave fleet of King Harry 'With silken Streamers, the young Phoebus fanning'; Iago's drowsy 'Not Poppy, nor Mandragora . . .'; Edgar's 'murmuring Surge,   That on th'unnumb'red idle Pebble chafes'; Macduff's summoning of trumpets, 'Those clamorous Harbingers of Blood, and Death'; the submarine profundity of Alonso's lament for his son who 'i'th'Ooze is bedded . . . deeper than e'er plummet sounded'. Always the sound, the actual combination of vowels and consonants, the long and the short, the quick and the slow, the sharp and the blunt, the heavy and the light weight—the sound itself is an enrichment of the sense.

It is not only the detail, but the long-range structure of Shakespeare's verse that requires study and practice from the executant. Much careful forethought and rehearsal, we may be sure, went into Burbage's handling of the *Long Paragraph*: even so expert a speaker as he must calculate the rising pitch, and avoid the common fault of ranting above the endurable compass of the voice:

> 'Tis not the Balm, the Sceptre, and the Ball,
> The Sword, the Mace, the Crown Imperial,

> The inter-tissued Robe of Gold and Pearl,
> The farced Title running 'fore the King,
> The Throne he sits on: nor the Tide of Pomp,
> That beats upon the high shore of this World:
> No, not all these, thrice-gorgeous Ceremony;
> Not all these, laid in Bed Majestical,
> Can sleep so soundly, as the wretched Slave:
> Who with a body fill'd, and vacant mind,
> Gets him to rest, cramm'd with distressful bread . . .

The sound of this passage is a long crescendo mounting in pitch and volume to a climax on the repeated phrase 'not all these', and descending in a deliberate anti-climax, the sound matching the sense as we come from the 'Bed Majestical' to the 'wretched Slave'. The revised pointing—'Nó, not all thése' changing to 'Not áll thesé'—clinches the moment of climax. Burbage might find the rise and fall of this passage comparatively easy to master: for the grammatical construction is foreseen in the speaker's mind from the start, and carried through to the end over a span of some twenty lines. Far harder is the disjointed syntax of King Lear's clamorous outburst under the nagging of his two daughters, just before he rushes out into the stormy dusk; the passage that begins 'O reason not the need . . .' and ends with the helpless cry of 'O Fool, I shall go mad'. Here the illusion to be created is not that of rhetorical climax but of the mounting incoherence of uncontrolled rage:

> No you unnatural Hags,
> I will have such revenges on you both,
> That all the world shall——I will do such things,
> What they are yet I know not, but they shall be
> The terrors of the earth!

The actor will plan this with exact calculation, but so as to give the impression of spontaneous improvisation, reserving the climax of pitch and volume for his final agonised appeal to the Fool.

And if Burbage bestowed much time and patience in practising such single speeches of King Henry and King Lear, his fellows joined him in the rehearsal and perfection of their ensemble-playing. There are duets, trios and quartets in which the *Long Running Rhythm* must be sustained. Even in his early plays, and increasingly in the great tragedies and later plays, Shakespeare's variation of pace and phrasing seems to be as vividly conceived and communicated as if he had marked his text with rallentando, accelerando, stretto, pause and cadence. Such duets are the scene between Macbeth and his Lady immediately after Duncan's murder: 'I have done the deed ...'; and Iago's patient and gradual seduction of Othello, with its studied (though seemingly improvised) rise and fall of intensity; and the passage where, with Desdemona all but dead in her bed, Othello unlocks the door to Emilia's urgent knocking. There is a trio for Hamlet, Horatio and Marcellus, to which Shakespeare himself contributes a fourth voice, swearing underground in the character of the Ghost. There is a quartet between Lear, Regan, Goneril and Cornwall (with trumpet-call and thunder thrown in), the passage which leads up to Lear's incoherent outburst. The quintet of the central storm-sequence—with five sharply distinctive voices, the King, the Fool, Kent, Edgar and Gloucester—has the character of an operatic ensemble, and the score is enriched with the instrumentation of thunder, wind and rain, judiciously timed and varied in pitch and volume by the back-stage men under the baton of the book-keeper.

Shakespeare's deliberate control of sound-effect is nowhere more remarkable than in his skill in *Gear-Change*—the subtle variations between verse-rhythms and prose. A MIDSUMMER NIGHT'S DREAM shows a constant change of time-signatures: the Fairies sometimes speak in tetrameters, the mortals in pentameters; there are rhyming couplets, and rhyming stanzas of six; there is blank verse for the energetic presentation of the lovers' quarrel; the mechanicals of course use prose, except when they show through their doggerel of 'Pyramus and Thisbe' Shakespeare's absolute command of caricature—and while the amateur players stumble through their halting verse, the hitherto impeccably metrical nobles detach themselves in the slick prose of dramatic criticism. TWELFTH NIGHT has a most delicate example, where Viola, in her first interview with Olivia, gradually lures that proud lady from mocking prose into romantic verse. A masterpiece of rhythmical manipulation used for pointing a scene of high comedy is the episode of Pistol's intrusion into Justice Shallow's orchard, where cousin Silence belies his name in full cry of drunken song; we hear the pawky dry tones of the factotum Davy; the raucous Bardolph; Pistol outrageous with his parody of tragic verse; Falstaff himself driven out of plain prose into an imitation of the swaggerer:

> O base Assyrian Knight, what is thy news?

and, as exuberant climax, the rhetorical iambics of Pistol's habitual rodomontade breaking through Shallow's pompous, stilted prose:

> Sir John, thy tender Lamb-kin, now is King,
> Harry the Fifth's the man . . .

The secret of that comic tour-de-force lies largely in the rich variation, between character and character, of speech-rhythms.

Meaningless incantation, the notorious verse-speaker's voice, was certainly not the habit of Shakespeare's company. But sometimes he asked them for a quality of *Cantando*—of singing tone—to render the deliberately lyrical passages by which he liked to induce a melting mood. There is nothing matter-of-fact in such a speech as this of the love-lorn Silvius in As You Like It: he is talking to the old shepherd Corin at his elbow, and assuming (as the young sometimes will) that the elderly know nothing about the state of being in love:

> If thou rememb'rest not the slightest folly,
> That ever love did make thee run into,
> Thou hast not lov'd.
> Or if thou hast not sat as I do now,
> Wearing thy hearer in thy Mistress' praise,
> Thou hast not lov'd.
> Or if thou hast not broke from company,
> Abruptly as my passion now makes me,
> Thou hast not lov'd.
> O Phebe, Phebe, Phebe.

The triple repetition, 'Thou hast not lov'd' (the line incomplete, left so deliberately by the poet), is a musical refrain, and was no doubt spoken as music. So too must all four speakers make music out of the melodious quartet from the same play:

> *Phebe*   Good shepherd, tell this youth what 'tis to love.
> *Silvius*   It is to be all made of sighs and tears,
>   And so am I for Phebe.
> *Phebe*   And I for Ganymede.
> *Orlando* And I for Rosalind.
> *Rosalind* And I for no woman.

The imitative sequence is twice repeated, and at the third utterance, by an elegant variation, the echo-phrase is lengthened: 'And so am I. . . .' And the spoken madrigal is pressed to a still musical conclusion with another echoed phrase:

> If this be so, why blame you me to love you?

Only when the irony of her disguise is too much for her composure, does Rosalind break the spell, which the verbal music has cast upon the playhouse, with an outcry (in prose):

> Pray you no more of this, 'tis like the howling of Irish Wolves against the Moon . . .

The mood is broken by deliberate mockery: it was not howling, but music that the two men and the two boy-players had concerted in sweet accord. In the last Act of THE MERCHANT OF VENICE Lorenzo and Jessica make a romantic prelude for Portia's home-coming with their repetition of 'In such a night. . . .' If Shakespeare's fellow-actors in such passages did not persuade their audience that they were listening to music, they were not doing what the poet asked of them. The actor who has no music in his soul—let no such actor be trusted with the text of poets.

*   *   *

Now in considering the vocal accomplishment of Shakespeare's fellow-actors—their command of the sense, the shape and the sound of his text—it may seem that we have overlooked their primary function, that of acting. An actor's job, it may be said, is to form a conception of the character he is playing, and to play it for all he is worth. This assumption (at least in reference to Shakespearian acting) is questionable. An enlightened critic once wrote about a Stratford Hamlet: 'He has not yet learned to trust Shakespearian verse, and believes it is possible to get through the part . . . by sheer acting: the result is disastrous.' As well might an opera be declared successful in all but the singing, or Brunnhilde think it possible to get through her part by sheer horsewomanship.

Yet this question of the representation of character in Shakespeare is an interesting one, and needs careful consideration: indeed only the comprehensive study of the plays in the conditions for which they were written would cover the whole range of Shakespeare's accomplishment, and that of his fellows, in this field. Although the mastery of sense, shape and sound was basic in the training of the Shakespearian company, there were other **Skills** required of them, and chief among these would certainly be the representation of individual character. No one would deny that Shakespeare has amply provided for this, in the only surviving part of his dramatic legacy—the spoken word of his actors. Indeed for the delineation of personality, as for all other dramatic purposes, the spoken word is Shakespeare's chief weapon. The physical skills of the actor (the assumption of a characteristic gait, or wheeze, or laugh, or a nervous tic, an expressive eyebrow, a palsied hand) undoubtedly contribute to the communication of individual character, no less than the false nose or the orange-tawny beard. But it is the speech above all which proclaims the man. Certain Shakespearian voices are unmistakable. With your eyes shut, through the subtle quality of the poet's phrasing, you would know who this is:

> Lock up my doors, and when you hear the drum
> And the vile squealing of the wry-neck'd Fife,
> Clamber not you up to the casements then,
> Nor thrust your head into the public street

To gaze on Christian fools with varnish'd faces:
But stop my house's ears, I mean my casements,
Let not the sound of shallow foppery enter
My sober house.

A very different personality splutters impatiently in these accents:

You swear like a Comfit-maker's Wife:
Not you in good sooth; and, as true as I live;
And, as God shall mend me; and, as sure as day ...
Swear me, Kate, like a Lady, as thou art,
A good mouth-filling Oath ...

And still a third voice is easily recognised in the unique pedantry of this:

If you would take the pains but to examine the Wars of Pompey
the Great, you shall find, I warrant you, that there is no tiddle
taddle nor pibble pabble in Pompey's Camp ...

There is no difficulty in detecting Mercutio, Falstaff, even Hamlet in his more intimate or astringent moods; there is less difficulty still in recognising the idiosyncratic speech of the 'character-parts' (in the modern sense of the phrase)—Justice Shallow, Corporal Nym, Mistress Quickly, the irascible old lord Capulet, Juliet's garrulous Nurse, Parson Evans, the Spaniard Armado, Holofernes the schoolmaster. No doubt justice was done to these eccentric impersonations, and if some were designed for the peculiar mannerisms of individual members of the company, we may nevertheless credit the Chamberlain's Men with a full measure of mimetic versatility. The skills required of Shakespeare's players, therefore, certainly included the ability to assume individual character with the voice; the characteristic idiom of Shylock or Hotspur or Fluellen must be matched with a characteristic inflection. One imagines too that a good deal of fun was had at those morning rehearsals, as one actor parodied the speech of another. William Sly's Hotspur is much addicted to mimicry: a general caricature of foppishness underlies his imitation of that 'Popinjay' who came to demand his prisoners on the battlefield; 'perfumed like a Milliner', with his snuff-box:

> . . . And still he smil'd and talk'd:
> And as the Soldiers bare dead bodies by,
> He call'd them untaught Knaves, Unmannerly,
> To bring a slovenly unhandsome Corpse
> Betwixt the Wind, and his Nobility.

But it is his colleague Phillips whom he guys, when he recollects with disgust and contempt the 'candy deal of courtesy' with which 'This fawning Grey-hound', King Henry (when he was mere Bolingbroke), once sought to enlist his support:

> Look when his infant Fortune came to age,
> And gentle Harry Percy, and kind Cousin:
> O, the Devil take such Cozeners . . .

For some such phrases he had heard Phillips himself utter in an earlier play of the cycle. And Burbage's Prince Hal is no less devastating in his satire on Sly's Hotspur who 'kills me some six or seven dozen of Scots at a Breakfast, washes his hands, and says to his wife; Fie upon this quiet life, I want work.' Even so Puck will assume the voices of his fellows, Demetrius and Lysander; Iago will caricature the tender tones of the gallant Cassio in the fiction of his dream (Verdi's bass appropriately adopts an uncanny falsetto for this malicious imitation). The skill of an assumed voice was not, of course, always directly imitative: Armin's brilliant mimicry found opportunity in his invention of the parson Sir Topas and in the rapid conversation between that prolix priest and his mercurial *alter ego*. Closely related to this accomplishment was the use of dialect—not only the skilful imitation of foreign idiom, such as the language of Captains Fluellen, MacMorris and Jamy, or the broken English of Doctor Caius, and of Princess Katherine and her Gentlewoman; but also the quadruple demand made of Condell's Edgar—as himself, as poor Tom o'Bedlam, as the rescuer of his father at the bottom of 'Dover cliff', and as the yokel deathsman of the serviceable villain Oswald: 'Chill pick your teeth, Zir: come, no matter vor your foins.'

Sometimes, in the conditions of this day-lit playhouse, with its Stage both broad and deeply thrust into the midst of the audience, the player was required to detach himself from the action and persons on the Stage and speak directly, in confidential address, to the audience. This device of speaking 'aside' needed a versatile manipulation of the voice, often sudden, sometimes in mid-speech; Shakespeare found ever new means of making the device effective. There is a primitive example in 1 HENRY VI, where Suffolk and Queen Margaret in extended colloquy each speak partly aside, but where at one moment Margaret, who has been largely unaware of the other's asides, nevertheless briefly overhears one of them. It is a far cry from this scarcely plausible scene to the self-communing of Macbeth, as he muses upon the 'supernatural soliciting' of the Witches, and his fellows observe from a distance 'how our Partner's rapt'. Edgar's asides, as he leads his blinded father from despair to acceptance, provide a continuous strand in the development of his part in the play, and amount almost to a running soliloquy both choric and self-revealing in its purpose. A whole chapter indeed might be written on Shakespeare's development of the familiar convention of soliloquy,[26] with its wide variety of style and method of approach to the audience, ranging from the informative address of Proteus through the philosophical brooding of King Henry the Fifth and Brutus to the impassioned self-revelations of Hamlet and the articulate conscience of Macbeth (each utterance of which is itself an episode in the course of the drama). The actors were expert in handling that delicate balance in which, while speaking still within the fictional framework of the role, they were nevertheless able to address the audience directly. This skill is typically a comic one, the art of the music-hall comedian who is able at will to step out of his assumed character. Shakespeare's use of it is sometimes comic, as when Launce buttonholes the audience to tell them of his dog Crab's antics; but this art of direct address seems at other times to have a serious purpose: Iago's soliloquies are a subtle combination of direct address ('And what's he then, that says I play the Villain?'), simple narrative exposition, interpretative comment and ambiguous self-revelation. In the Epilogues of Puck and Prospero, it is hardly possible to tell where the player is speaking and where the character.

Many of these skills are not the exclusive property of the Shakespearian actor, and there were others, too, common to accomplished performers in almost all ages—and not only of the legitimate drama. Physical agility and grace were no doubt taken for granted. In many scenes the players must be skilled swordsmen: the contests between Hal and Hotspur, Hamlet and Laertes, Edgar and Edmund, Coriolanus and Aufidius, were too important to the dramatic effect of the play to be amateurish scuffles: but scuffles there were in plenty in the *excursions* of battle-scenes, which required an energetic and disciplined disorder from numbers of minor actors. The player of Orlando must show some skill in wrestling. Prince Arthur must make a spectacular leap to death from the upper level. Clowning involved the tumbler's art. And there were many dances of all kinds, in an age of expert dancing, not the least athletic being the dance of the twelve herdsmen in THE WINTER'S TALE who could jump 'twelve foot and a half by th'square'. Musical accomplishment, as we have seen, included singing and the playing of various instruments.

Nevertheless we must never forget that Shakespeare expected of his colleagues in the playhouse not only the conventional skills of the actor but also the special arts demanded by the poetic drama of which he was the greatest master. We have considered briefly the communication through speech of individual personality; it seems that in many of Shakespeare's great acting roles the expression of personality is less vivid than in the peripheral 'character-parts' (Macbeth, for instance, is certainly not as Scotch as Captain Jamy). The individual character-sketches, as Shakespeare leaves them to us, are fewer in number than is generally supposed; and they belong mainly to his early maturity, and become fewer as his art develops to its ultimate expressiveness. The belief dies hard that characterisation was the first item in Shakespeare's dramatic plan. But when we study the plays in the conditions for which they were composed, we soon reach the conclusion that it was only one of other features, which are at least equally important. We do not suggest that there is nothing distinctive in speech to identify, for instance, Lear or Othello; the strong-willed incoherence of the one and the controlled grandeur of the other are palpably distinctive, but much more is involved: Shakespeare's conception, while it is richer than mere symbol, is deeper and more universal than mere character. The great acting roles of Shakespeare's maturity are more closely woven into the textural unity of their plays than most of their predecessors, and some roles there are (Prospero, for instance, or the Duke in MEASURE FOR MEASURE) whose personality seems almost wholly to have been subordinated. Shakespeare developed as a dramatist; but in all his plays, from the early chronicles and comedies to the great tragedies and last plays, he demanded more from his colleagues than mere character-studies.

THE POET-PLAYWRIGHT

If we consider what else Shakespeare expected of his actors, we must return in imagination once more to the interior of that playhouse and the conditions of circumstance and personnel we have sought to establish in the early chapters of this book; and in so doing we shall come nearer to understanding the nature of the poetic drama itself, and especially of the unique achievement of Shakespeare in this field. We are groping after a discovery of the miracles of illusion that took place in Shakespeare's playhouse. Every time that an audience thronged into the Yard and the Galleries of that Wooden O, they were confronted with the same sight—the broad deep Stage jutting out into the centre of the building, and the Tiring-House behind it, in the steady neutral daylight of the London afternoon. Each time the focus of their interest was the question, what will they turn it into today? On the bare and unlocalised Stage it is often necessary to inform the audience of where the action takes place; for while many scenes have no particular locality, many others inevitably require it. This problem is not difficult of solution: a communicative Chorus can tell us 'unto Southampton do we shift our Scene'; question and answer may provide the information ('Barkloughly Castle call you this at hand?'—'Yea, my Lord'), or Rosalind's simple statement, 'Well, this is the Forest of Arden.' By what they say and do, the players can always plant us without difficulty where the playwright wants us to be. But the poet's task is more subtle, not only to inform us of place but also to convince us of atmosphere. Such is Shakespeare's craft that the atmosphere is created within a few minutes of the play's start. His means is poetical: that is to say, the medium of his illusion is the spoken word: this is the Poet's Method. In the first scene of JULIUS CAESAR a simple phrase identifies place: 'Why dost thou lead these men about the streets?' But then he builds upon this factual foundation:

Triumph . . . Conquest . . . Tributaries . . . Chariot Wheels . . .
Walls and Battlements . . . Tow'rs and Windows . . . Chimney
tops . . . Tiber trembled underneath her banks . . . Run to your
Houses . . . Go you down that way towards the Capitol . . .
Caesar's Trophies . . .

These are some of the phrases which fix our imagination firmly in the
streets of Rome. Two speakers, whose characters are hardly distinguishable one from the other, begin to convert the humdrum
setting of the playhouse into the mercantile splendour of maritime
Venice:

> Your mind is tossing on the Ocean,
> There where your Argosies with portly sail
> Like Signors and rich Burghers on the flood . . .

Metaphor mingles with reality, for Signor Antonio their companion
is a rich burgher, whose argosies are tossing on the ocean:

> I should not see the sandy hour-glass run,
> But I should think of shallows, and of flats,
> And see my wealthy Andrew dock'd in sand,
> Vailing her high top lower than her ribs
> To kiss her burial . . .

These actors are not engaged in sheer acting: they fulfil, with their
talk of maps and ports, spices and silks, and pageants of the sea, the
poet's purpose of transforming the atmosphere of the playhouse. In
play after play, Shakespeare performed this initial miracle. Detailed
examination of the opening of HAMLET will show how, within fifty
lines, we are chilled to the marrow by the sight of a Ghost in full
armour on the battlements of a castle at midnight. Sometimes atmosphere is created without locality: at the beginning of OTHELLO a
world of circumstance is created for the play before we become
gradually aware that we are in the streets of a sleeping city. Nor is it
only at the start of a play that the atmosphere must be created. Often

in the course of the story a special need arises. In ROMEO AND JULIET Stage and Tiring-House become, at different times, a torch-lit dancing-party, a moon-lit garden, a sultry afternoon in the streets:

> The day is hot, the Capulets abroad:
> And if we meet, we shall not scape a brawl,
> For now these hot days, is the mad blood stirring . . .

and for the tragic end, a graveyard:

> Under this Yew-tree lay thee all along,
> Holding thy ear close to the hollow ground,
> So shall no foot upon the Churchyard tread,
> Being loose, unfirm with digging up of Graves,
> But thou shalt hear it . . .

Phrase after phrase in this melancholy scene builds up the atmosphere of the churchyard:

> . . . how oft tonight
> Have my old feet stumbled at graves . . .

and leads us to what Romeo has described as a 'detestable maw', a 'womb of death', the inset of the Tiring-House, where Juliet lies en-tranced:

> What Torch is yond that vainly lends his light
> To grubs, and eyeless Skulls? As I discern,
> It burneth in the Capels' Monument.

In A MIDSUMMER NIGHT'S DREAM the moonlit, fairy-haunted darkness, which has itself been created by insistent poetical imagery, must at last be dispelled. It is a technical achievement worth noting: the Duke and Duchess enter to the jolly music of the hunting horns, and their phrases evoke the cheerful rising of the sun—'the vaward of the day . . . the Western valley . . . up to the Mountain's top . . .' and the hounds whose

heads are hung
With ears that sweep away the morning dew . . .

The prolonged conversation (it runs to some 25 lines) contributes
little to character-drawing or plot: but it is a theatrical necessity to
bring daylight (strange irony) into the daylit playhouse. A rare moment
of peaceful contentment in MACBETH is needed for Shakespeare's
ironical purpose: for King Duncan, approaching his general's castle at
Inverness, knows nothing of the treachery that awaits him there. The
actor (it may have been the poet himself) immediately transforms the
Tiring-House into 'This Castle' with its 'pleasant seat'. And then that
skilled player Lowin, as Banquo, seems to watch the flight of a bird
from the sky above the thatched roof of the playhouse to perch in the
recesses of the façade: and the other actors on the Stage follow his
gesture as he gives substance to the poet's words:

This Guest of Summer,
The Temple-haunting Martlet does approve,
By his loved Mansionry, that the Heaven's breath
Smells wooingly here: no Jutty frieze,
Buttress, nor Coign of Vantage, but this Bird
Hath made his pendent Bed, and procreant Cradle:
Where they most breed, and haunt, I have observ'd
The air is delicate.

It is a passage of great beauty, but it throws no light on the character
of the speaker: indeed, if we had time to reflect, the ornithological
interest might seem incongruous in the mouth of Macbeth's fellow-
general. Nevertheless the dramatically ironic purpose is clear enough,
since the King's hostess (who enters on this line) has been heard in the
previous scene, a few moments before, to say:

The Raven himself is hoarse,
That croaks the fatal entrance of Duncan
Under my Battlements.

Lowin's task, as he well knows, is to create the atmospheric background for the poet's effect of tragic irony.

The atmospheric conditions are constantly evoked in the speech of the actors, not only in the great set-pieces but pervasively in passing word and phrase. Thus Romeo beneath Juliet's window transforms the whole playhouse with his evocation:

> Lady, by yonder blessed Moon I swear,
> That tips with silver all these Fruit tree tops . . .

The picture in the mind's eye is objectively clear. Brutus, in his garden on the stormy night before the Ides of March, tells us:

> I cannot, by the progress of the Stars,
> Give guess how near to day . . .

and then, since he must read the anonymous letter which he holds in his hand:

> The exhalations, whizzing in the air,
> Give so much light, that I may read by them.

A little later in the scene, one of the conspirators informs us that

> yon grey Lines,
> That fret the Clouds, are Messengers of Day.

The clock, interrupting the whispered conference of the conspirators, strikes three. When Portia comes, Brutus chides her for committing her

> . . . weak condition, to the raw cold morning.

Many of these atmospheric lines are famous, and justly so, for their beauty:

> how still the evening is,
> As hush'd on purpose to grace harmony.

How sweet the moon-light sleeps upon this bank,
Here will we sit . . .

But look, the Morn in Russet mantle clad,
Walks o'er the dew of yon high Eastern Hill . . .

The need to create the atmosphere breeds the poetry, but conversely the poetry comes into its own when it is actually doing what it was devised for. There is a danger, on a stage where visual illusion is an important consideration, that some of Shakespeare's atmospheric effects may seem mere superimposed ornament (lovely, lyrical stuff, but to be got through, hurried or even—for purposes of dramatic vigour—cut). And just because it is paradoxical, it must be emphasised that the very attempt to use mechanical means and gimmicks extraneous to the poet's conception, to help him out, as it were, to put his meaning across, is disastrous: for the poet has done all that was required by appealing not to the eye, but to the mind's eye. It is to the mind's eye (the phrase is Shakespeare's own, in HAMLET, I.ii.185) that the playwright and his fellow-actors address themselves: 'Work, work your Thoughts, and therein see. . . .' This was Shakespeare's challenge to his audience, and the challenge is still there, if we will take it up. If the audience does not form the habit of seeing with the mind's eye, then the poet's work is in vain. But the habit once formed, the whole audience (galleries and groundlings and all) will recognise the immense power of Shakespeare's poetry to create dramatic illusion.

Sometimes, when his intention is to invest the Stage and Tiring-House with a particular locality, the visible features play a part in the process: 'Go to the rude Ribs of that ancient Castle . . .' says Bolingbroke to his envoy, and the Tiring-House immediately acquires the substance of Flint Castle. So too is Macbeth's castle at Inverness brought before our eyes in the words of Duncan and Banquo. Shylock's door, Oliver's door, Brabantio's door (with his window above it) have a like objective reality, and the doors of Gloucester's house which are shut up to exclude King Lear in the stormy night. But there is an important converse proposition to this habitual practice of investing the Stage with the necessary character, atmosphere and locality. Since there is no attempt at visual illusion, and the Tiring-House, whatever its composition, is permanent, habitual and therefore readily ignored, there are times when the poet will expect us to abandon any conception of locality at all. There are many scenes which take place nowhere in particular: the focus of our attention is entirely upon person and circumstance. Of such a kind are THE MERCHANT OF VENICE, II.viii, where Salarino and Salanio describe the rage of Shylock and the tender parting of Bassanio and Antonio; the scene of the Welsh Captain in RICHARD II, II.iv; and ANTONY AND CLEOPATRA, III.v, a dialogue between Enobarbus and Eros which records the fading of Lepidus from the triumvirate. Moreover, the unlocalised stage makes it possible for the playwright to create a sense of locality for the moment and as quickly abandon it when it has served his purpose. OTHELLO, IV.ii, seems to begin in the chamber of Desdemona (the jealous husband's morbid fancy that Emilia is porteress of a brothel has the greater dramatic force when we see that Desdemona's private apartment is the venue of the scene): but it ends with a conversation between Iago and the mutinous Roderigo: only in the naturalistic theatre is it necessary to create some device by which this disappointed suitor may plausibly seem to find his way into Desdemona's chamber.

There are times indeed when the poet will want us to travel in the mind's eye far from the immediate place and circumstance of his play. A clear illustration of this can be seen in that passage of JULIUS CAESAR in which Cassius is persuading Brutus to join the conspiracy. As we have seen, Shakespeare has skilfully established that the action takes place in the streets of Rome; but it is in the nature of the poetic drama on the unlocalised stage that one locality can be established, as it were, within another. In his anxiety to prove that Caesar is no better a man than themselves, Phillips, the eloquent Cassius, presents a vivid picture of an episode in their past association. He makes his audience shiver on that 'Raw and Gusty day'; they hear the waves lapping against the river-banks, 'The troubled Tiber, chafing with her Shores'; they realise that it is Caesar who offers the challenge; they fix their eyes on 'yonder Point', and see Cassius plunge in first, 'Accoutred as I was';

they feel the effort of the struggle with the roaring torrent, as the two swimmers

> did buffet it
> With lusty Sinews, throwing it aside,
> And stemming it with hearts of Controversy.

Next moment, we are present at a different scene (different, but very apt for comparison):

> I (as Aeneas, our great Ancestor,
> Did from the Flames of Troy, upon his shoulder
> The old Anchises bear) so, from the waves of Tiber
> Did I the tired Caesar . . .

Now Phillips would not be doing his job, if we did not at the moment feel that he is carrying an old man on his shoulders out of the blazing ruins of a sacked city. And even then the poet has a further demand: work, work your thoughts, and therein see a picture of Caesar shivering with a fever on his Spanish campaign, pale and groaning, and crying 'Give me some drink Titinius, As a sick Girl.' The difference between Shakespeare's (and Phillips's) method and that of his present interpreters can be seen if we envisage the dilemma of the film-director in presenting this scene. Instead of the rapidly shifting focus of Shakespeare's spoken vision, what can we expect of the camera-man (impatiently enduring the protracted length of the speech) except a series of angle-shots of Brutus and Cassius backed by irrelevant vistas of Roman architecture? The swimming-match, the sack of Troy and the sick-bed in Spain are all part of the texture of the poet's play, and it is because of the neutrality of the ever-familiar Stage and Tiring-House that poet and actors can so easily carry the imagination of their audience elsewhere. Similarly, it is essential that the actor, and we with him, should be detached from all surroundings, when Macbeth, just before going to murder Duncan, intensifies our sense of darkness and evil with image after image:

Now o'er the one half World
Nature seems dead, and wicked Dreams abuse
The Curtain'd sleep . . .

Shakespeare wants us to think of Duncan's curtained sleep—shut up in measureless content; and of Banquo's wicked dreams—'Merciful Powers' (it was his bedtime prayer), 'restrain in me the cursed thoughts That Nature gives way to in repose.'

. . .Witchcraft celebrates
Pale Hecate's Off'rings . . .

We remember the Weird Sisters, hand in hand:

. . . and wither'd Murther,

(in posture and gesture and movement, Burbage is himself this personified Murder)

Alarum'd by his Sentinel, the Wolf,
Whose howl's his Watch, thus with his stealthy pace,
With Tarquin's ravishing strides,

(as the actor allusively remembers that other secret crime, his own gait recalls the prowling criminal)

towards his design
Moves like a Ghost.

This masterpiece of horrifying suspense needs (for the moment) to be detached from all background save what is visible to the mind's eye, prompted by the poet's words. Thereafter the two clinking strokes of the little bell (his wife's reminder that 'my drink is ready'—the coast is clear) remind Macbeth, and us, that we are on the way to the King's bedchamber.

*　　　*　　　*

Against his background of atmospheric illusion (not only the immediate background of locality but also the richer texture of imagery) Shakespeare created certain figures, which are now universally famous. We all have our memories of this or that performance—Lang's Othello, Ainley's Antony, Ayrton's or Wolfit's Lear, Malleson's Aguecheek, Gielgud's Hamlet or Benedick, Olivier's Richard or Hotspur, Redgrave's Berowne, Ashcroft's Queen Margaret, Vanessa Redgrave's Rosalind or Ronald Pickup's, Atienza's Fool. What we sometimes forget—and it needs saying—is that there exist prototypes of all these roles, the characters which Shakespeare intended, and which are fully drawn in the printed texts of the Quartos and Folio. We have once again to remind ourselves that almost the whole of Shakespeare's legacy is in the words which he gives to his actors to speak. There are none of those italicised character-studies which Bernard Shaw prefaces to the entry of his characters; none of those directive adverbs by which a playwright of today indicates how he would like his words spoken; the stage-directions which portray the appearance and demeanour of the actors are few and far between. Yet when it is important that we should have an intimate acquaintance with the persons of Shakespeare's plot, the information is full and detailed in the words of the prompt-book.

And here we must remember again the uncompromising neutral daylight of the London afternoon in which the plays were performed. The effect of this was quite different from what we are used to in the theatre of today; an effort of the imagination is needed to recreate the very tang and taste of the open air. Hodges writes of birds flying down into the Yard in the evening to pick up the crumbs left by the afternoon audience. 'If this sounds,' he continues, 'merely a picturesque sentimentality, consider nevertheless what a very different setting it conveys in reality.' From the point of view of the audience, it would be like sitting to watch the tennis-championships on the centre-court at Wimbledon, where part of the crowd is under cover, but quite a large proportion of 'groundlings' under the open sky; the game itself in the open air. There we have this great concentration of a crowd upon certain individuals active in their midst: we cannot really see the shifting expressions on their faces (as we could if we were watching them in grease-paint under theatre-lights, or through the microscopic lens of the movie-camera); but we are acutely aware of their movements and gestures, and if they are (like actors) of the demonstrative kind, we shall understand their moods, we shall feel with them—the agony of a series of match-points, the frustration of a linesman's doubtful decision. We shall find ourselves groaning aloud in sympathy, protesting audibly, and when our champion scores a point giving vent to our elation in spontaneous cheers.

But there is a difference. What happens on our tennis-court is predictable: we know the rules, and the plot is stereotyped and repetitive: it needs no further interpretation than the monotonous pronouncements of the umpire: we know right from the start what the principal actors are trying to do. But as we sit in the top gallery of the Globe, we don't know at all what is going to happen: we don't even know who the principal figures are that sally forth from the two great Doors or from the central curtains: we may recognise Burbage by the trick of his voice, or Pope by a familiar mannerism, or Heminges by his stuttering, circumlocutory speech, or Cowley whose spindly legs (like two such riding rods) admit of no disguise; but we do not know who they are meant to be today, until they are introduced to us by their own words or by some other actor's description. Not only their general character but their momentary demeanour is often described: Brutus, aside to Cassius on the perimeter of the Stage, delineates the embarrassment of the group who have emerged from the farther Door:

> The angry spot doth glow on Caesar's brow,
> And all the rest, look like a chidden Train;
> Calphurnia's Cheek is pale, and Cicero
> Looks with such Ferret, and such fiery eyes
> As we have seen him in the Capitol
> Being cross'd in Conference, by some Senators.

Burbage directs the eyes of the audience; in the daylit playhouse, where the deliberate directing of light was not possible, the playwright's words act as a moving spot-light or as the travelling camera of the cinema, selecting first one point of focus, then another. But the poet is able to go beyond description to interpretation. And it is a pervasive practice of Shakespeare's, not confined only to the central persons of his play. The 'Goose-look' of an unnamed messenger is vividly interpreted to us by Macbeth. In the same play, our attention is drawn to the first appearance of Rosse, by the interpretative words of one of his fellow-thanes:

> What a haste looks through his eyes!
> So should he look, that seems to speak things strange.

We have a vivid momentary glimpse of Iago's hypocrisy when Othello bids him give an account of the brawl he has himself engineered to get Cassio into trouble:

> Honest Iago, that looks dead with grieving,
> Speak: who began this?

This same device of word-painting plays its part in making the death of Desdemona unbearably painful. Bending over her, as the boy-actor lies asleep in the curtained space in the middle of the Tiring-House wall, Burbage speaks of

> that whiter skin of hers, than Snow,
> And smooth as Monumental Alablaster . . .

(one thinks of the recumbent figures on the great tombs in the Beauchamp Chapel at Warwick—no distant journey for a native of Stratford-upon-Avon). Then, later in the scene, when she is dead, and (too late) he realises her innocence:

> Now: how dost thou look now? Oh ill-Starr'd wench,
> Pale as thy Smock: when we shall meet at compt,
> This look of thine will hurl my Soul from Heaven,
> And Fiends will snatch at it. Cold, cold, my Girl?
> Even like thy Chastity.

Beside these two 'close-ups' of Desdemona, we may set two more of
Othello himself. As he bends over her in bed, her terrified voice says:

> . . . you're fatal then
> When your eyes roll so . . .

and asks him:

> Alas, why gnaw you so your nether-lip?
> Some bloody passion shakes your very Frame.

These descriptive phrases are an essential part of the stagecraft of this
playhouse: they are the means by which we not only see but also read
the features of Othello, in his momentary posture not easily visible to
the physical eye of the audience.

As so often, dramatic necessity bred dramatic opportunity. We have
seen already how in the hands of this poet-playwright character often
expresses itself in distinctive speech, and it is by an extension of the device of word-painting that our apprehension of character is deepened.
All that Cassius says and does contributes to our understanding of him,
and this understanding has already been directed by the poet:

> Yond Cassius has a lean and hungry look,
> He thinks too much . . .
> . . . that spare Cassius. He reads much,
> He is a great Observer, and he looks
> Quite through the Deeds of men. He loves no Plays,
> As thou dost Antony: he hears no Music . . .

And instead of Bernard Shaw's long italicised description attached to the
character's name on his first appearance, we have this:

> Seldom he smiles, and smiles in such a sort
> As if he mock'd himself, and scorn'd his spirit
> That could be mov'd to smile at any thing.

This, in the medium of the cinema, would be represented simply by the subtle facial expression of the actor in close-up. Shakespeare's close-ups (of which there are plenty) are of necessity verbal ones: for the subtlety of facial expression cannot be seen in his playhouse—certainly cannot be seen by more than a handful of his audience at any one moment.

We do not of course suggest that there is always a simple correlation by which verbal descriptions of a character are merely developed in his own words and actions. A complex interrelation between what we see a person doing and hear him saying, what he says of himself, and what the other persons (with whatever purpose, objective, benevolent or in malice) say of him, is made possible by use of the verbal instrument: and it is this complexity which creates the character. In the first scene of OTHELLO the playwright deliberately deceives his audience with a vivid and, it seems, complete picture of his central character (whom we have not yet seen); apart from the grudging admission that the State has need of his generalship, our impression of Othello is wholly unpleasant: he is a pretentious soldier, 'loving his own pride', weak in his judgement of men, and above all barbarously coarse: the Moor (so he is contemptuously named throughout the scene) is 'Thick-lips . . . an old black Ram . . . a Barbary horse . . . gross . . . Lascivious . . . an extravagant, and wheeling Stranger. . . .' This repulsive impression is immediately belied by the natural dignity of Othello's first utterances. We know (there is no doubt about it) what he has done; but his midnight marriage with Desdemona, so scabrously depicted by Iago, is put into a different perspective by his own noble apologia before the Duke in council. Our response to Othello cannot be simple. Through the foolish Roderigo and the grief-stricken Brabantio, as well as the malicious Iago, the poet has set in motion a complex interplay of response and interpretation. In ANTONY AND CLEOPATRA the words and actions of Mark Antony himself create a character which is at various times vain, cruel, obstinate, petulant and besotted; and yet our final impression of him is undeniably one of personal greatness. Only a full analysis of the play in the conditions for which Shakespeare wrote it will show how greatly the poet's skilful use of the verbal instrument contributes to this paradoxical impression, from the opening lines of the play when Philo not only comments on 'this dotage of our General's' but remembers how 'his goodly eyes ... Have glow'd like plated Mars', to the moment near the end of the play when Cleopatra dreams of 'an Emperor Antony'.

*   *   *

Now if Phillips's Cassius and Burbage's Othello needed this kind of verbal support to bring their characterisation to fullest dramatic effect, much more was involved in creating the illusion of feminine personality. We may be in doubt about many of the physical features of the Elizabethan theatre, but there is no escaping from the circumstantial fact that the women's parts—Viola, Portia, Rosalind, Beatrice, Ophelia, Cressida, Lady Macbeth, even Cleopatra—were written to be performed by boys. It should be said at once that there was no question here of clumsy incompetence—the sort of thing that was hinted at in Olivier's film of HENRY V. It is surely unthinkable that the verbal subtlety and quick wit of Rosalind would have been written as it was, if the young player of this part had been 'a great lubberly boy'; and the very fact that their author is not afraid to make direct reference to the transformation is testimony to his confidence in the boy-actors' bringing it off. The most audacious challenge to the disbelief of the audience is offered when Cleopatra, envisaging the circumstances of Caesar's triumph, imagines how her love for Antony will be guyed in the Roman playhouses:

> ... Antony
> Shall be brought drunken forth, and I shall see
> Some squeaking Cleopatra Boy my greatness ...

The passage would never have been penned so, unless the boy-Cleopatra in Shakespeare's playhouse was indeed great. The playwright was confident, no doubt, in the skill of the particular boys that were available at the time of writing: and how lucky we are that John Edmans's voice was not 'crack'd within the ring' the year after his Lady Macbeth; had it been so, would the poet have dared to embark on the infinite variety of Cleopatra?

The boy-player's task will seem a little less formidable, if we re-member that it was in no way unusual: since all female parts in the public playhouses were taken by boys, none had the effect (as they would today) of a special theatrical device or ephemeral gimmick. Inevitably Shakespeare sometimes exploited, most often for comic or ironic purposes, the boy-girl's ambivalence of gender: it is indeed the genesis of the favourite trick of disguise. And he was uncompromising about this too: Portia, for instance, says to Nerissa:

> I'll hold thee any wager
> When we are both accoutred like young men,
> I'll prove the prettier fellow of the two,
> And wear my dagger with the braver grace,
> And speak between the change of man and boy,
> With a reed voice, and turn two mincing steps
> Into a manly stride ...

It is an impudent bluff on Shakespeare's part, and would indeed be a foolish one, if the boy-speaker were not to seem at this moment a woman mischievously relishing the prospect of a masquerade. Although Shakespeare is not averse to exploiting this ambivalence, the audience must ultimately be made to feel that the disguise is no more than a disguise and that the boy-player is indeed a woman. The moment comes in As You Like It when Orlando is wearied by the 'idle talking' of Ganymede; when at the end of the play Ganymede, like Twelfth Night's Cesario, becomes woman again, the harmonious restoration of order depends upon the audience's whole-hearted acceptance of the fact. So complete is this acceptance that in the jeu d'esprit of Rosalind's Epilogue ('If I were a Woman . . .') they can be mocked by the boy-player for their ready susceptibility to illusion.

In considering Shakespeare's dramatic craftsmanship, then, we must not forget his skill in creating the illusion of womanhood. Apart from the available talent of his boy-players, and the prevalence of a theatrical convention by which he could rely on the audience's ready acceptance, he had another reason for confidence—it was his best—namely his dramatic poetry, which could not only transform his stage, and fill the neutral afternoon with stormy midnight, but could also create the illusion of womanhood in the person of a boy.

It becomes necessary to repeat once again that all that has survived of these extraordinarily subtle characters (a whole gallery of portraits, each different in her kind) is the printed text of Folio and Quarto—that is, the words which the actors are to speak. The charming sincerity of Viola does not exist apart from the spoken text. The Duke, Olivia, Malvolio, all contribute to the impression we form of Viola, but none so eloquently as her brother Sebastian who thinks her drowned:

> A Lady sir, though it was said she much resembled me, was yet of many accounted beautiful: but though I could not with such estimable wonder over-far believe that, yet thus far I will boldly publish her, she bore a mind that envy could not but call fair . . .

And every word that she herself speaks confirms the judgement. The feminine qualities of the character are created not only by the 'sheer acting' of the boy-player but also by the poet's word which deepens and enriches it. The less amiable charm of Cressida is likewise reinforced by the spoken word: Troilus and Pandarus introduce her to us before she ever appears; and Ulysses's shrewd portraiture sums up her promiscuity:

> There's a language in her eye, her cheek, her lip;
> Nay, her foot speaks, her wanton spirits look out
> At every joint, and motive of her body . . .

She is (as he cynically puts it) one of the 'daughters of the game'.

The most complex and complete of Shakespeare's heroines is, of course, Cleopatra. We can only assume that in his boy-player (Baldwin suggests that it was John Edmans) the playwright found a performer of unusual vocal and emotional range, who could express, with equal skill, majesty, flirtatiousness, quick wit, barbarity, pathos, ennui, sensual passion and many other moods both direct and subtle. Only a continuous exposition of the play's performance in Shakespeare's playhouse (where the verbal instrument was allowed its purposed activity) could attempt to cover the various facets of that incalculable personality. It need hardly be repeated that they emerge partly out of the speech of Cleopatra herself, and partly out of the web of comment, description, reminiscence and narrative that Shakespeare, through the other characters, has built round her. No other female character in his plays is so often, or so fully, brought before the mind's eye of the audience. She would be much less real, much less complete, to us, without Enobarbus's cynical admiration, Caesar's articulate disapproval, the inquisitive gossip of the Romans. The great set-pieces of description are justly famous but, as always, the poet's method is pervasive. Enobarbus's account of her first meeting with Antony upon the river of Cydnus is immediately followed by an epilogue of reluctant praise:

> I saw her once
> Hop forty Paces through the public street,
> And having lost her breath, she spoke, and panted,
> That she did make defect, perfection,
> And breathless pow'r breathe forth.

At the beginning of the play, the cynical Enobarbus predicts the violence of Cleopatra's reaction to Antony's proposal of leaving Alexandria: he has often seen her 'die' for far less momentous reasons:

> I do think there is mettle in death, which commits some loving act upon her, she hath such a celerity in dying.

Later, Cleopatra speaks of her skin, darkened by the sun, as 'with Phoebus' amorous pinches black'. At the end of the play these two sensual images are fused into one, as Cleopatra welcomes in fact the approach of death:

> The stroke of death is as a Lover's pinch,
> Which hurts, and is desir'd.

Thus the unrelated facts of extravagant grief, sunburn, and the ultimate experience of death are integrated in imagery which itself helps to create the illusion of feminine personality. Towards the end of the play a further dimension is added to this infinitely various character in the themes of marriage (for in death Antony is her 'Husband') and motherhood, which find a climax in a moment of great tenderness: while Plutarch continually insists that the target of the deadly asp was Cleopatra's arm, Shakespeare deliberately followed another tradition: his Cleopatra applies the asp to her breast:

> Peace, peace:
> Dost thou not see my Baby at my breast,
> That sucks the Nurse asleep . . .

The composite portrait which John Edmans has presented is now a 'Lass unparallel'd'.

Just as Shakespeare's poetry is needed to animate the neutral architecture of the playhouse, to project pictures, as it were, upon a blank screen, so also did the poet use the boy-player, with all the vocal and physical skills that such a boy could command, to project living character upon the neutrality of his blank screen. Now in something the same way as an attempt at visual realism (like that of the camera-man in the film of JULIUS CAESAR) will positively obstruct Shakespeare's spell, which is addressed through the ear of his audience to their mind's eye, so there is a danger that the real femininity of the great actress in her maturity will obscure the clear outlines of Shakespeare's poetical portrait. It may be that the fundamental reason is a psychological as well as a physiological one: the mature actress has at her command an emotional force and power of personality which is altogether outside the range of the adolescent boy. It will be her instinct to use it to the full, and if she does, she will obscure and obstruct Shakespeare's makebelieve which seeks to create its effect through the ear and the mind's eye of the audience. That is precisely why Shakespeare did not write into the love-scenes of, for instance, ROMEO AND JULIET and ANTONY AND CLEOPATRA those scene-stopping clinches which are the staple attraction of cinema romance. The physical expression of love which he from time to time required on his stage is not an exercise in its own right, but is always so calculated as to serve the larger interests of the play. To allow the use of that full range of feminine personality which is available to the great actress, and which was no part of Shakespeare's conception, is to distort the balance of the play as he so carefully and indeed so inevitably poised it.

One important thing, certainly, about the female parts is that the perspective of their place in the drama should not be out of focus. The Shakespearian actress who now plays the parts is truly great when she remembers that they were written for boys and that, because of this circumstantial fact, there is no place in Shakespeare's conception for the star performance which overweights the structural balance of the play. A boy, if he cut up rough, put on airs, said he could not make his effects unless he had the centre of the stage, could be laughed out of his sulks, or chidden, or even spanked. Prospero and Ariel give us the model:

> How now? moody? . . .
> If thou more murmur'st, I will rend an Oak
> And peg thee in his knotty entrails, till
> Thou hast howl'd away twelve winters.

If, as we have previously suggested, it is part of the poet's scheme that Lady Macbeth should walk in her sleep 'above', because the whole of the last Act thereby gains shape, then the boy could be put in his place (literally, up aloft) and taught how to make his effects potent from up there. John Edmans could be spanked; and the book-keeper would scarcely have hesitated to peg him, if not in the entrails of an oak, at least in the confines of the Chamber. The responsible actress, who has inherited his task, will surely need less persuasion to accommodate 'sheer acting' to the Poet's Method.

*   *   *

Word-painting, then, is an important element in the poet's method both in projecting atmosphere and in creating character; we have seen moreover that for this latter purpose the poet will often go beyond description to interpretation. If we proceed to observe that this is no less true in his atmospheric creation, we shall begin to understand how it is that each play exists in a world peculiarly appropriate to itself. The atmosphere it seems is not merely palpable or physical (as in the realistic theatre the dimming of stage-lights indicates the approach of darkness), but in the working of its imagery part of the unity of the play. Macbeth evokes the atmosphere not only of dusk but also of ruthless evil as, commanding the playhouse from the upper level, he calls on the 'seeling Night' to

> Scarf up the tender Eye of pitiful Day . . .

And immediately, on the Stage below, 'Night's black Agents' in the form of his hired assassins creep stealthily forth to waylay Banquo on his way to the King's feast. One of them, looking out into the play-house at horizon level, says:

> The West yet glimmers with some streaks of Day.
> Now spurs the lated Traveller apace,
> To gain the timely Inn . . .

It is this actor's task not only to bring down the twilight over the bare Stage but also to make dramatic capital out of the fear that twilight brings for the benighted traveller: there is much force in the word 'timely': we in the audience all want to be under the shelter of some hospitable roof, we all fear for the safety of Banquo and his young son, as they walk through one of the Stage-Doors (no door at this moment) and the echo of their retreating horses' hooves still sounds in our ears.

A series of examples will show how Shakespeare was progressively less content with simple descriptions but learnt to interpret for his audience their dramatic effect. The prelude to the battle of Shrewsbury is a dialogue between King Henry and his son:

> *King* How bloodily the Sun begins to peer
> Above yon busky hill: the day looks pale
> At his distemperature.

Prince   The Southern Wind
Doth play the Trumpet to his purposes,
And by his hollow whistling in the Leaves,
Foretells a Tempest, and a blust'ring day.
King   Then with the losers let it sympathise,
For nothing can seem foul to those that win.

By a direct use of the pathetic fallacy, the pallor of the blustering day
becomes obviously but effectively prophetic of the coming conflict.
The stormy portentous night before the Ides of March is described
in objective detail by the anxious Casca, but confident Cassius interprets its relevance to the development of Shakespeare's theme:

Now could I (Casca) name to thee a man,
Most like this dreadful Night,
That Thunders, Lightens, opens Graves, and roars,
As doth the Lion in the Capitol . . .

Most movingly, in the last Act of the same play, when Cassius lies
dead on the very front of the Stage, his friend Titinius kneels beside
the body, looks out at horizon level (in the afternoon daylight of the
Globe) and says:

O setting Sun:
As in thy red Rays thou dost sink to night;
So in his red blood Cassius' day is set.
The Sun of Rome is set. Our day is gone,
Clouds, Dews, and Dangers come . . .

These lines of Titinius (spoken by a minor member of the company)
epitomise the unique power of the poetic drama, designed expressly
for, and only to be fully realised upon, the bare Stage of Shakespeare's
playhouse. The lighting expert can lay on a red cyclorama at this point,
and make-up can imitate the red blood of the dead Cassius: but only
the poet can fuse the two in an image of despair which colours the whole
of the play's last Act. The sun of Rome is set.

The classic example of such interpretative description is the storm-sequence which is the central arch of the mighty architecture of KING LEAR. A full exposition of the play in performance will analyse the way in which the different but related sufferings of the Fool, Edgar, Gloucester and Kent evoke the storm in the daylit playhouse, and above all the means by which Burbage's Lear can both help to create the storm through his gargantuan invocation of the elements and at the same time suffer in it as 'A poor, infirm, weak, and despis'd old man'. But we may meanwhile notice that the very opening phrases of the sequence suggest the line of our interpretation:

—Who's there besides foul weather?
—One minded like the weather, most unquietly.

The unquiet mind of the anonymous Gentleman is an early step in the process by which, in the sequel, the poet keeps us constantly aware of the tempest in Lear's mind which

Doth from my senses take all feeling else,
Save what beats there, Filial ingratitude . . .

Before he ever appears in the storm, we are given elaborate guidance to interpret his demeanour. This Gentleman has the important task of prompting our reaction, when the moment comes: not only does he draw a vivid picture of the old King 'Contending with the fretful Elements', but also he provides a memorable interpretation of what he has just seen, and we shall shortly see, how the King

Strives in his little world of man to outscorn
The to and fro conflicting wind and rain . . .

Moreover we understand the Fool's antics better when we remember the Gentleman's answer to Kent's question:

—But who is with him?
—None but the Fool, who labours to out-jest
His heart-struck injuries.

*   *   *

Macbeth's conjuring up of darkness and the Gentleman's preview of
Lear in the storm provide examples of another recurrent habit of
Shakespeare's poetic drama: interpretative description or narrative
sometimes anticipates what we are about to see, so that we may read
more into the subsequent action or appearance than we would without
such a preface; the mind's eye is, as it were, set to work in anticipation.
Before Ophelia's first mad scene, Horatio gives us this sympathetic
guidance to our reaction:

> She is importunate, indeed distract,
> Her mood will needs be pitied . . .
> She speaks much of her Father; says she hears
> There's tricks i'th'world, and hems, and beats her heart,
> Spurns enviously at Straws, speaks things in doubt,
> That carry but half sense: Her speech is nothing,
> Yet the unshaped use of it doth move
> The hearers to Collection; they aim at it,
> And botch the words up fit to their own thoughts,
> Which as her winks, and nods, and gestures yield them,
> Indeed would make one think there would be thought,
> Though nothing sure, yet much unhappily.

Nothing could be clearer than that we are being asked, in advance, to
read between the lines of Ophelia's mad utterance. Examples can be
multiplied of this habit of anticipation. Romeo's first entry is prefaced
by two extended speeches—from Benvolio and from his father Monta-
gue—portraying the secretive melancholy of the conscious lover.
Viola's obstinate determination to penetrate Olivia's privacy is re-
counted at length with sour wit by the Lady's frustrated Steward
before she sets foot in her presence. We are prepared by the description
of Lucilius and by Brutus's interpretative comment—'A hot Friend,
cooling'—for the resentment of Cassius which erupts into the famous
scene of the quarrel. When Albany's gentle reserve turns at last to
outraged condemnation of his wife Goneril's cruelty, we have a
warning glimpse of his changed demeanour: Oswald describes him to
his mistress:

... never man so chang'd:
I told him of the Army that was Landed:
He smil'd at it. I told him you were coming,
His answer was, the worse ...
... he call'd me Sot,
And told me I had turn'd the wrong side out:
What most he should dislike, seems pleasant to him;
What like, offensive.

Such preliminary promptings seem to arise from the conditions of the playhouse, with no bright light concentrated on the faces of the actors, with the story taking place in the midst of the audience, who sat or stood in the same neutral light, not watching a detached picture, but assisting at events, a crowd on the fringes of sensational action. Their ears tell them more than their eyes. Work, work your thoughts, and therein see ... but the imagination needs helping, and part of Shakespeare's method is to describe and interpret what we must feel we see on his Stage (action, circumstance, character, locality, atmosphere), and by anticipation to make sure that the audience respond in the way his purpose demands.

Not only does he anticipate, but often he presents a scene for the second time in retrospect. Few of the precisely sumptuous details in Iachimo's reminiscent description of Imogen's bedchamber can actually have been visible on the Stage when he stole from his hiding-place; his evocation of the rare and beautiful enriches in retrospect a scene we have already witnessed. Where the poet's recreative description deals, as it so often does, with action, we live the experience over again: for the vivid speech and evocative miming of the actor re-creates what we have already seen, and in the process directs our reaction to it. Our pleasure is doubled in the process of repetition. So Puck recounts for his master's entertainment the headlong flight of the mechanicals at sight of Bottom's translation. Re-enacting the scene on the same Stage (for visually it looks the same) where we have just witnessed it, he reminds us by position and gesture of the very moment when, in answer to Thisbe's line, from the hawthorn-brake which was Peter Quince's choice for their tiring-house, 'forth my Mimic comes'. In reminiscence, as he speaks of thorns and briars, the illusion of the forest which Shakespeare has been at such pains to create, is confirmed in the mind's eye. The panic stampede is enriched with metaphorical comparison:

> As Wild-geese, that the creeping Fowler eye,
> Or russet-pated choughs, many in sort
> (Rising and cawing at the gun's report)
> Sever themselves, and madly sweep the sky:
> So at his sight, away his fellows fly . . .

and these images too are evoked with illustrative mime and gesture, and clapped hands to make the gun's report. In a different vein, Benvolio, at the Prince's command, reports the details of the fray in which first Mercutio and then Tybalt have been slain. His account is as graphic as the action itself, and carries us once again through the anxious emotions of that sudden and headlong catastrophe. The recollection, when we have had time to ponder the tragic issue of the event, gives to the action double dramatic weight. We have something of the same experience when we witness on the television screen the replay of a match of which we already know the result: there is much to be observed and enjoyed in watching (in slow motion, perhaps) the process of victory and defeat, the presence of mind of the winner, the courageous endurance or humorous resignation of the loser. The highway robbery at Gad's Hill, recollected in the comparative tranquillity of the Boar's Head tavern, extracts full measure of comedy from that visually comic episode: both Falstaff's brilliant improvisations and Prince Hal's plain factual tale add new dimensions to the spectacle we have already enjoyed. Iago's account of Cassio's drunken brawl has a special flavour from the diabolical hypocrisy of the narrator: fascinated, we hear how damning is his evidence against the lieutenant, and yet how fairly his tale records the facts; so fairly indeed that Othello can say of it:

> I know Iago
> Thy honesty, and love doth mince this matter,
> Making it light to Cassio . . .

While we listen to the delivery of this tale, we admire of course the skill of Lowin's rendering of Iago's hypocrisy. But he is also fulfilling another of Shakespeare's purposes—to interpret the violent indiscipline, which we have just seen enacted, as it must appear to the judgement of Othello newly roused from the intimacy of his first night of marriage. It is the effect upon Othello which gives this retrospective narration its full dramatic force. The effect is made verbally: it is a device characteristic of Shakespeare's poetic drama.

* * *

The Poet's Method creates a world in the playhouse, by interpretation as well as description, by anticipation and reminiscence, as well as by direct representation; but this is not all: the audience which has formed the habit of listening and reacting to the kind of poetry which gives a local habitation to the airy nothing of Shakespeare's fancy will fall into closer attention and absorption, and begin to people the playhouse with pictures beyond the visible illusion of place and persons. We shall see what takes place elsewhere and at other times. Another recurrent habit, then, of Shakespeare's poetic drama is the use of what may be called creative narration or description. This process takes many forms and has different purposes; but there is one constant feature: the narrative is itself an episode in the play's action, and must be realised by the actor in performance. Cassius must make us see each moment of his swimming-match—the plunge, the struggle in the water, the rescue. The bleeding Sergeant in the second scene of MACBETH must embody in word and gesture the battle which begins the play, must himself show us how Macbeth 'carv'd out his passage, Till he fac'd' the rebel Macdonwald, must himself enact the ruthless vigour of that stroke which 'unseam'd him from the Nave to th'Chops'; only when he has fulfilled his task of creative narration may he seem to feel the severity of his own wounds, those 'Gashes' which 'cry for help'. The amount of miming and posture and gesture will depend upon the content of the story: but Shakespeare's colleagues, we may guess, were not slow to use expository illustration in putting across to their audience the vivid pictures of the poet's text. The boy who played Ophelia, for instance, has an important narrative: if the audience do not envisage the action he describes, the play lacks an essential episode in Shakespeare's plot. It is not difficult to imagine the gestures with which the boy brings his tale to life: Ophelia is sewing in her closet: the Prince bursts into her presence; his doublet is all unbraced, his stockings are hanging about his ankles, his face is distraught:

> He took me by the wrist, and held me hard;
> Then goes he to the length of all his arm;
> And with his other hand thus o'er his brow,

(the word 'thus' is evidence of a gesture)

> He falls to such perusal of my face,
> As he would draw it . . .
>   . . . That done, he lets me go,
> And with his head over his shoulder turn'd,
> He seem'd to find his way without his eyes,
> For out o'doors he went without their help;
> And to the last, bended their light on me.

For the duration of this tale, we in the audience are not concerned with a conversation between Polonius and his daughter: with the mind's eye we see the strange actions and demeanour of Hamlet, as the boy-player presents them to us in lively mime.

Not less important is the story of the origin of that little flower which causes such havoc in the hearts of the Athenian lovers in A MID-SUMMER NIGHT'S DREAM. Here Oberon tells us a strange tale of supernatural fantasy, and the boy Goffe's gestures point its simple geography. Immediately above his head is 'the cold Moon', under his feet 'the earth'; 'Flying' in from the topmost Gallery on one side of the playhouse comes 'Cupid all arm'd'; on the other side at the level of the Stage is the 'fair Vestal, throned by the West'; we are made to see Cupid loose 'his love-shaft smartly from his bow', and the arrow's flight abruptly checked as it is 'Quench'd in the chaste beams of the wat'ry Moon'; we observe the stately and unruffled progress, as

. . . the imperial Vot'ress passed on,
In maiden meditation, fancy free.

And then Goffe shows us how 'the bolt of Cupid' plummeted to earth
at his feet, landing upon

a little western flower;
Before, milk-white; now purple with love's wound,
And maidens call it, Love in idleness.

Meanwhile his voice, with carefully varied rhythm, lends fire and pace
to Cupid's shaft, a moment of dramatic incident in the onomatopoeic
word 'Quench'd', and unruffled majesty to the heedless Virgin Queen.
With such an origin, so vividly evoked, the magic flower acquires the
potency to control both mortals and immortals in the sequel. Shakespeare does not hesitate to use his method of creative narration and
description for episodes or scenes of the first importance to the action
of the play—the death of Falstaff, for instance, or the climactic meeting
in which Leontes rediscovers his lost daughter; it is hard to realise
that we never see with the physical eye the chamber where Duncan
lies in his blood, guarded by the snoring grooms, so compelling is the
gradual accumulation of detail which paints this picture for us.

*   *   *

How closely woven, for all its astonishing range and variety, is the
texture of this poetic drama, will appear in another feature which
recurs in many of Shakespeare's mature works—a feature which, for
want of a better phrase, we may designate the echo-method. Words,
phrases and themes which are of importance in his treatment of his
story are echoed up and down the whole course of the play. KING
LEAR provides several illustrations of this device. Cordelia's blank
'Nothing' in response to her father's irrational demand has more than
one clear echo in the Fool's bitter wit, which at least once teases the
King into involuntary recollection of his initial folly:

—. . . can you make no use of nothing Nuncle?
—Why no Boy,
  Nothing can be made out of nothing.

Sometimes the effect is anticipatory, a kind of pre-echo preparing us for what is to come. The storm is hinted at some time before we hear the first sounds from the back-stage men. The fugitive Edgar, in soliloquy, declares how he will

  with presented nakedness out-face
The Winds, and persecutions of the sky . . .

Lear, in the presence of Regan and Cornwall, invokes upon the head of the absent Goneril 'All the stor'd Vengeances of Heaven', and cries:

  You nimble Lightnings, dart your blinding flames
  Into her scornful eyes . . .

The theme is repeated, when Goneril arrives to reinforce her sister's insolent cruelty:

  Return to her? and fifty men dismiss'd?
  No, rather I abjure all roofs, and choose
  To wage against the enmity o'th'air . . .

And Lear's choice of phrase is no accident (it may indeed have been the first cue for the back-stage symphony) when he says to Goneril:

  I do not bid the Thunder-bearer shoot,
  Nor tell tales of thee to high-judging Jove.

More striking still is the trail of preparation Shakespeare lays for that other climactic action in the same play, the blinding of Gloucester. Lear, in his anger against Goneril's determination to make him dis-quantity his train, rebukes the weakness of his age which makes him weep:

Old fond eyes,
Beweep this cause again, I'll pluck ye out,
And cast you with the waters that you loose
To temper Clay.

A similar image underlies his misplaced confidence in his other daughter:

When she shall hear this of thee, with her nails
She'll flay thy Wolvish visage.

And on the brink of his martyrdom, Gloucester, still unaware of the nature of his imminent fate, answers the third-degree inquisition of his tormentors, as they clamour to know why he has sent the King to Dover:

Because I would not see thy cruel Nails
Pluck out his poor old eyes . . .

It seems that our imagination must become acclimatised to the horrible image of savage blinding before the event itself.

Just such a running theme is the insistent echo of the 'deed' to be 'done', which projects the conflict of hesitation and resolution in the opening Acts of MACBETH: the verbal repetitions of 'do', 'done', 'deed', are a deliberate device of the poetic drama, working to a culmination in the murderer's stark announcement 'I have done the deed'; and the force of this particular echo rings right through the play until the agonised cry of the sleep-walker, 'What's done, cannot be undone.' Such a serial emphasis has the quality of a musical leit-motiv, and is no more to be slurred over in performance by the actors, than the recurring themes of Wagner's *Ring*.

The subject of pervasive imagery in Shakespeare has been discussed at length and from different points of view. We are not concerned here with the light that it has seemed to throw upon the poet's personal tastes and interests, or the literary expression of his subconscious thought-processes, but rather with the use he made of this resource in the composition of his plays. W. H. Clemen, in his book on *The Development of Shakespeare's Imagery*, makes clear how consciously the poet employed this artifice for his dramatic purpose, and how his use of imagery developed and became more various in effect and intention during the course of his career. Close analysis of the plays in performance will give opportunity to study many examples. One thing can be stated in advance of such an analysis (and indeed it is not a surprising thing), that there is no single formula of purpose to cover them all. In early days, the poet used pervasive imagery for the immediate purpose of creating atmosphere: the many images of moonlight in the opening scenes of A MIDSUMMER NIGHT'S DREAM prepare us in advance for the transformation of the bare Stage into a fairy-haunted wood. The purpose is primarily atmospheric, but the images are part of the texture of the play: remove one of them (for instance, Hippolyta's comparison to 'a silver bow, New bent in heaven', or Theseus's mention of 'the cold fruitless Moon', or Lysander's fancy of how 'Phoebe doth behold Her silver visage, in the wat'ry glass, Decking with liquid pearl, the bladed grass'), and the spell which Shakespeare is accumulating is weakened. RICHARD II is a milestone in the poet's progress to maturity in that the subtle and pervasive use of imagery not only expresses the temperament of the King himself but also establishes the harmonious unity of the play. The moral ambivalence of the central dilemma in JULIUS CAESAR is brought constantly to our mind's ear in the persistence of antithetical imagery. Clemen persuasively shows how in OTHELLO Shakespeare's use of imagery projects character (not static but in dynamic change) with greater depth and subtlety than the surface mannerisms of speech which helped to create his earlier 'character-parts'. In KING LEAR it is not enough to say that the insistent imagery of violence done to the body, of the elements, of the world of animals and nature, has a purpose of direct symbolism; it is more deep-rooted than that: it creates the huge and terrible universe in which the play exists. The imagery of disease in HAMLET, of blood or darkness or sickness in MACBETH, of the sea in THE TEMPEST, has often been analysed and expounded; only in the flexible conditions of that playhouse which bred Shakespeare's poetic drama can it be seen in practice to fulfil its various dramatic purposes.

* * *

The conclusion we are reaching towards is a reconsideration of the very nature or essence of Shakespeare's drama in performance, and a resultant reappraisal of the actor's task in interpretation. If we were to envisage a manual of studies for the Shakespearian actor, it would be easy to compile the first phase of instruction from such examples of sense, shape, sound and other skills as we have suggested above. And when our Shakespearian company—the new Chamberlain's Men—had mastered this first part of their course, we should look forward to their rendering, with the pleasure of the connoisseur savouring in advance the subtleties of an operatic score; and we should enjoy in their performance not only the loving expression of familiar details but also points of phrasing and interpretation which we have never heard before and hear with delight now for the first time—as if the ink were still wet on the stave.

But, as we have seen, a consideration of the actor's task leads us to re-examine the method of the poet in the playhouse: and we must, it seems, develop a further course of study, the composition of which is less easy to define. If we were asked what was that extra accomplishment demanded from the virtuoso of Shakespeare's poetic drama, we should have to summarise it as the *realisation* (the bringing before the mind's eye of the audience) *of all the pictures* conjured up in the text. We use the word 'pictures' in a comprehensive sense, not always of precise and concrete visualisation (though this is often the case); the appeal of Shakespeare's imagery is not, of course, confined only to the sense of sight, but is aimed at the other senses too and beyond them to a total and clearly focused apprehension, emotional, intellectual and associative. It is in this comprehensive way that Shakespeare is of all poets the most pictorial. The picture may take the form of pure narrative, as in Ophelia's description of the distraught Hamlet, or Oberon's history of the little western flower. It may take the form of extended character-sketching, as Caesar fills in the portrait of Cassius with the lean and hungry look. It may be a matter of atmospheric description, as Banquo's murderer induces the twilight in which the lated traveller spurs apace to gain the timely inn. It may be exact and concrete in its appeal, as when Celia tells how she found Orlando 'under a tree like a dropp'd Acorn', or it may take an abstract form, as in Hamlet's catalogue of the whips and scorns of time:

> The Oppressor's wrong, the proud man's Contumely,
> The pangs of dispris'd Love, the Law's delay,
> The insolence of Office, and the Spurns
> That patient merit of the unworthy takes . . .

In voice and gesture Burbage will bring to full dramatic life each miniature experience of the series. It may be a thumb-nail sketch, like one of the Seven Ages of Man:

> the whining School-boy with his Satchel
> And shining morning face, creeping like snail
> Unwillingly to school . . .

or that shrewd caricature (from TROILUS AND CRESSIDA) of the

> fashionable Host,
> That slightly shakes his parting Guest by th'hand;
> And with his arms out-stretch'd, as he would fly,
> Grasps in the comer . . .

(a passage that implicitly demands expressive gestures of parody from the speaker). It may be figurative imagery—a simple phrase as when King Richard speaks of Bolingbroke as being set on by pride

> To wake our peace, which in our Country's cradle
> Draws the sweet infant breath of gentle sleep . . .

A finger to the lips and a glance at an imaginary cradle help to bring the metaphor before our eyes, as if with voice and gesture (Hush, don't wake the baby!) the King were indeed protecting a sleeping child from dangerous disturbance. The picture may be embodied in a single word, so easily overlooked when we take for cliché what is precise expression, as when Hamlet decides to observe his uncle:

> For I mine eyes will rivet to his Face . . .

In the course of his training in the art of literal description, the actor may perhaps have come across the armourers of HENRY V, 'with busy Hammers closing Rivets up'; he may toy too with the memory of Iachimo, whose keen tongue clinches the metaphorical use of this word with a gloss:

> Why should I write this down, that's riveted,
> Screw'd to my memory . . .

Image may follow image in rapid change, so as to create tumultuous intensity of feeling; thus Macbeth imagines the consequence of Duncan's murder in the famous passage of soliloquy which evokes the transcendental pictures of Angels trumpet-tongued, the babe Pity striding the blast, and Heaven's Cherubin horsed upon the sightless couriers of the air. Or the swift accumulation of related images may fulfil a single purpose; thus Leontes expresses his agony of mind as 'Goads, Thorns, Nettles, Tails of Wasps'. The picture may be an extended image, like that in which the sick King Henry the Fourth addresses Sleep who will not visit his sick-bed:

> Wilt thou, upon the high and giddy Mast,
> Seal up the Ship-boy's Eyes, and rock his Brains,
> In Cradle of the rude imperious Surge,
> And in the visitation of the Winds,
> Who take the Ruffian Billows by the top,
> Curling their monstrous heads, and hanging them
> With deaf'ning Clamours in the slipp'ry Clouds,
> That with the hurly, Death it self awakes?

Canst thou (O partial Sleep) give thy Repose
To the wet Sea-Boy, in an hour so rude:
And in the calmest, and most stillest Night,
With all appliances, and means to boot,
Deny it to a King?

In this example we can see clearly the alternatives before the player. 'Sheer acting' will present us with a sick man feebly murmuring on his death-bed, asking for a glass of water and a couple of aspirin tablets. But then we shall not see this portentous storm at sea, and the boy blissfully unaware at the mast-head; we shall not feel the turmoil of the King's spirit or the still night of his sick-room in which he lies awake. The storm and the boy are part of the texture of the poet's play, and the virtuoso speaker will not allow us to miss them.

When the actors who have mastered the whole compass of our imaginary manual bring the substance of Shakespeare's drama, its constantly shifting subject-matter—narrative, description, comment, philosophical speculation, meditation, characterisation, emotional interaction, symbol, metaphor, wit, rhetoric, word-play, irony—clearly before the mind's eye of the audience, then indeed comes in the millennium; then from their lips we shall hear and feel and understand— spoken in due sense, shape and sound—the words which are the chief instrument in the fulfilment of Shakespeare's dramatic purpose. The task is a demanding but not impossible one. In the conditions for which Shakespeare wrote the instrument is allowed to fulfil its purposed function; in his playhouse the swift continuity, the close texture and the architectural shape of his plays can be fully realised; the devices of sight and sound, which were part of his conception of each play, can take their proper place in the balance of its performance. The director's task is demanding too; not the imposition of extraneous elements of design and production, nor the selecting and developing of single aspects of a play, but the comprehensive interpretation in performance of the author's complex and various conception. And from the audience the poet-playwright demands a positive, creative collaboration: in the most often quoted exposition of the Poet's Method, he explicitly and insistently invites this working collaboration:

And let us . . .
On your imaginary Forces work . . .
Work, work your Thoughts, and therein see . . .
      . . . But now behold,
In the quick Forge and working-house of Thought . . .

But the demands made upon actor, director and spectator unquestionably bring their reward: it is in the fulfilment of them that the whole world of Shakespeare's play comes into being in the playhouse.

That Shakespeare himself well understood the nature of this collaboration between speaker and hearer cannot be doubted; and there is incidental support for this view in that he did not hesitate to make an explicit demonstration of its use a turning-point in the narrative of one of his plays. It is a clear illustration of the Poet's Method, as if the conjuror for once did his sleight of hand with his coat off, so that we could see the mechanics of his trick. The scene is in the fourth Act of KING LEAR, and besides being a tour-de-force of illusion, it is a profoundly moving episode in the story. Edgar, still disguised as a Bedlam beggar, is leading his old father, now cruelly blinded. The old man has asked him, in an earlier scene, to conduct him to

    a Cliff, whose high and bending head
Looks fearfully in the confined Deep:
Bring me but to the very brim of it . . .
          . . . from that place,
I shall no leading need.

There is no mistaking his suicidal purpose. The patient, faithful Edgar has decided to play a trick upon his blind father: in an 'aside' he explains to us why:

    Why I do trifle thus with his despair,
Is done to cure it.

He does not bring his father to the cliff; but his purpose is to persuade Gloucester that he has done so. The ground is as 'even' as Gloucester thinks. He cannot 'hear the Sea', because the sea is not there. And Edgar needs all his ingenuity of mime and gait to feign a steep climb: 'Look how we labour.' At first Gloucester seems unconvinced, but Edgar leads him forward to the centre of the Stage:

> Come on Sir,
> Here's the place: stand still . . .

And after this sharp note of warning, the creative process begins:

> how fearful
> And dizzy 'tis, to cast one's eyes so low,
> The Crows and Choughs, that wing the midway air
> Show scarce so gross as Beetles. Half way down
> Hangs one that gathers Samphire: dreadful Trade:
> Methinks he seems no bigger than his head.
> The Fishermen, that walk upon the beach
> Appear like Mice: and yon tall Anchoring Bark,
> Diminish'd to her Cock: her Cock, a Buoy
> Almost too small for sight. The murmuring Surge,
> That on th'unnumb'red idle Pebble chafes
> Cannot be heard so high.

The sockets of the old man's blind eyes follow each detail of the description. Edgar's final pretence of dizziness communicates itself to his imagination, and through his to ours:

> I'll look no more,
> Lest my brain turn . . .

A further step forward, to 'within a foot' (again the sharp note, warning of danger) 'of th'extreme Verge', and we are ready to 'Topple down headlong'. So Gloucester falls from the cliff of his imagination to the bare boards of the Stage. In pursuit of his illusion, the versatile Edgar (Henry Condell, part-editor of the Folio) changes his role for the second time—a new voice, a new personality. He has become a passerby on the beach at the bottom of the cliff, hurrying to aid the stranger who has just fallen 'From the dread Summit of this Chalky Bourn'. His pretended ignorance of Gloucester's predicament is ingeniously assumed: 'Look up a height . . . Do but look up.' Again the poet's atmospheric invention sustains the pretence. Both eye and ear are prompted to imagine the height of the fall:

> Ten Masts at each, make not the altitude
> Which thou hast perpendicularly fell . . .
> Look up a height, the shrill-gorg'd Lark so far
> Cannot be seen, or heard . . .

It is 'a Miracle' indeed that the old man is alive, no bones broken, can even stand up. The final stage in Edgar's plan is easy, to persuade his father that poor Tom, who led him to the top of the cliff, was a devil. Therefore his miraculous salvation is the work of 'the clearest Gods', no longer, it seems, playing with his life like wanton boys with flies. The trick has worked: Gloucester's despair is, for the time being at least, cured:

>   henceforth I'll bear
> Affliction, till it do cry out it self
> Enough, enough, and die.

A timid director, fearing that the audience may laugh, will hanker after a step or a rostrum for this scene, so that Gloucester may have some 'cliff' to fall from. *There is no cliff*—save on the tongue of Edgar and in the eyes of Gloucester. Yet the cliff is high enough to cure the blind man's despair. Edgar's stratagem is not only a trick of illusion, but it works upon the spirit too. The parallel with Shakespeare's own art is easy to see. While Gloucester is the listener, Edgar is the poet-dramatist, working with gesture, posture, demeanour, miming, and above all with the spoken word upon our imaginary forces, and upon the spirit too.

*   *   *

We have not attempted in the foregoing pages to make an exhaustive examination of the nature of Shakespeare's dramatic craftsmanship. Only by reconstructing, in imagination or in fact, the conditions of performance in his own playhouse can we appreciate to the full the power of his dramatic poetry to fulfil its purposed function. The great variety of Shakespeare's achievement (no one play repeating the style or content of another) makes it impossible to reduce his method to stereotyped formula; and it is our intention, in the subsequent volumes of the series to which this is a preface, to follow individual plays through from start to finish, reconstructing (by reasoned conjecture) those early performances of Shakespeare's lifetime. Meanwhile, we hope that we have made clear the grounds of our belief that his text is continually dramatic in conception, so that no scene, no speech, no line of it can be jettisoned without careful consideration of the part it plays in the fulfilment of the playwright's purpose, nor adequately performed except by a careful study of its effect in the context of the play and in the conditions of the playhouse for which it was written; the plays are masterpieces in the form in which they are recorded for us in the early printed texts, needing far less adaptation, improvement, refinement or coarsening modernisation than is often implicitly assumed to be necessary before they can make their full impression upon the imagination of an audience of today. Their medium is the poetic drama, of which Shakespeare the poet-playwright was the supreme master. He was moreover a player himself; and he knew how to make a play.

NOTES

Page 34
1   The figures on the upper level of the Swan drawing have been variously interpreted as actors or audience: perhaps the most interesting suggestion is Nagler's, that what De Witt saw was a rehearsal in progress; he points out that the drawing shows no other audience, and adds that he is 'inclined to regard them as actors or, at any rate, theatre personnel, who were following the rehearsal from the gallery and perhaps waiting for their cue' (*Shakespeare's Stage*, 10 f.). But there is no reason to suppose that De Witt intended to represent either a performance or a rehearsal: his expressed purpose in making the drawing suggests that it is diagrammatic and that the figures are inserted for the normal descriptive or symbolic needs of a diagram.

2   The reader who would like to consult the Swan drawing or the Fludd engraving will find them both reproduced in Andrew Gurr's *The Shakespearean Stage, 1574–1642*; and there is a comprehensive collection of the pictorial evidence in Hodges, *The Globe Restored*. In her thought-provoking book, *Theatre of the World*, Frances Yates includes a discussion of the Fludd engraving and its implications, and also a suggested sketch, based upon her discussion, of the Globe Stage and Tiring-House. Dr. Yates argues that James Burbage and his successors were fulfilling a more conscious and elaborately conceived aesthetic purpose in the building of the public playhouses than has hitherto been recognised.

Page 35
3   The reader who wishes to sample some other kinds of written evidence should turn to W. W. Greg, *Dramatic Documents from the Elizabethan Playhouses*. A selection of stage-directions from the early printed texts is to be found in King, *Shakespearean Staging 1599–1642*.

Page 39

4 Richard Hosley in his article 'The Use of the Upper Stage in *Romeo and Juliet*' (*Shakespeare Quarterly*, 5, 371 ff.) analyses the relationship between the two versions on the premise that, while the Second Quarto was mainly printed from Shakespeare's 'foul papers', or manuscript, the First Quarto 'represents our play *after* production and therefore may reflect production alterations necessary to stage the foul-papers text . . . in an Elizabethan public theater'. Hosley rejects the independent use of the upper level, and argues that the Q2 text is defective: 'Undoubtedly Shakespeare intended the action of III.v to shift from the upper to the lower level, but apparently in writing out his foul papers he either failed to visualize the staging problem posed by the transition of scene or left the details of staging to be worked out in rehearsals. . . .' It is unlikely that Shakespeare would have written (and the Folio editors printed) a version of the scene impracticable in the playhouse. Any denial of the extended and independent use of the Chamber in this episode must involve considerable emendation not only of the stage-directions but also of the dialogue printed in Q2 and the Folio: as Hosley observes, 'It is ironic that the foul-papers text of the transition requires adaptation for Elizabethan production but not for a "modern" one.' It is ironic indeed: in Elizabethan production, if we assume the extended and independent use of the Chamber, no adaptation at all is needed.

Page 40

5 To the reader who doubts whether this manoeuvre was possible, we can only answer that we have demonstrated empirically, in public performance, that it was so: with boy-players enacting the Ladies' parts, and no equipment other than ropes, Antony was drawn into the Chamber some 12 feet above the ground. The final stage-direction, *Exeunt, bearing of Anthonies body*, need not be taken to imply that there were no curtains or hangings which could be drawn to conceal the Chamber: if, as we suspect, a shallow area of the Chamber projected beyond the curtains (for use, perhaps, as battlements when the whole Chamber was not revealed), it would still be necessary to carry the body behind the 'curtain-line'. In any case, the drawing of curtains is by no means incompatible with the moving spectacle of the Ladies bearing away the body of the dead General.

Page 46

6 The suggestion of placing the scenes of the sub-plot on the upper level was made by J. C. Adams in an article on 'The Original Staging of *King Lear*'

(*Joseph Quincy Adams: Memorial Studies,* Folger Shakespeare Library, 1948); this disposition has been tested in productions of the play at Harrow, at the University of Colorado, Boulder, and at Haddo House, Aberdeen, on each occasion with manifest effect in clarifying the complicated narrative.

Page 50

7 E. K. Chambers supplies the bare record of facts about Shakespeare's fellow-actors; T. W. Baldwin provides the fullest account of their organisation as a company and their individual identity. An easily digestible account of the part they played in the poet's achievement can be found in a chapter on 'The Players' in M. M. Reese's *Shakespeare.*

Page 55

8 The reader is referred to Bertram Joseph's *Elizabethan Acting* (second edition, 1964) for an illuminating discussion of the subject. Particularly interesting are the illustrations of rhetorical gestures of the hand taken from John Bulwer's *Chirologia* and *Chironomia* (1644). Daniel Seltzer, in *A New Companion to Shakespeare Studies,* 35 ff., has some balanced comments on the acting-style of the time; and there is an interesting chapter on 'The Players', which also includes a discussion of the acting-style, in Gurr, *The Shakespearean Stage 1574–1642.*

9 Gurr (75) quotes Campion's attack on old-fashioned players: '... if they did pronounce *Memeni,* they would point to the hinder parts of their heads, if *Video,* put their finger in their eye. But such childish observing of words is altogether ridiculous.' He also instances a student-play from Cambridge, which includes the stage-direction: *He acts it after the old kinde of Pantomimick action.*

Page 56

10 Both the writers of this volume have been associated with a company of amateur players who, meeting no more than once a year, rehearse and perform a play of Shakespeare (on an Elizabethan stage) in four or five days. It is the group-feeling of the company and the continuous tradition of many years that makes coherent performances possible in such conditions. The acting-style of the Old Harrovian Players has developed (by evolution over the 21 years of the company's existence) from the exigencies of playing Shakespeare in the conditions for which he made his plays.

Page 57

11 These and other pictures which may suggest the costumes of the play-houses can be found in Hodges.

Page 58

12 M. Channing Linthicum, *Costume in the Drama of Shakespeare and his Contemporaries*, includes, among other things in a very full examination of the time, a discussion of colours and their symbolism. It is not easy to deduce the existence of standardised conventions; but if, for instance, we may believe that yellow was indicative of hope of marriage, the joke of Malvolio's stockings becomes the richer.

Page 75

13 Beckerman, *Shakespeare at the Globe*, 179 f., persuasively argues (supporting his contention with both quotation and deduction) that 'entrance of actors through the enclosure curtains was not unusual, and, in fact, may have occurred more frequently than we usually assume'. The full examination of Shakespeare's plays in performance will show how certainly he is right.

Page 79

14 Coghill, *Shakespeare's Professional Skills*, 16.

Page 83

15 The reader who wishes to consider this aspect of Shakespeare's stagecraft in further detail will find much to interest him in Naylor, *Shakespeare and Music*, and in Noble, *Shakespeare's Use of Song*. A concise account of the various uses for which Shakespeare employs music can be found in Watkins, *On Producing Shakespeare*, 62 ff. There survive several instrumental pieces and vocal settings likely to have been used by Shakespeare's company; a comprehensive collection of the music used after the accession of James I in 1603 is printed in Cutts, *Musique de la Troupe de Shakespeare*; Naylor, *Shakespeare Music*, includes not only some of the vocal and instrumental music certainly used in Shakespeare's plays, but also other music of the time which is appropriate for use in performance. For sound-effects other than music, the reader is referred to Shirley, *Shakespeare's Use of Off-Stage Sounds*.

Page 84

16 Cutts argues that, in the public playhouses at least, the provision of a particular 'music room' did not begin to become customary until towards the end of Shakespeare's life.

Page 92

17 The reader is referred for the general topic to E. K. Chambers, *William Shakespeare*, I, ch. V; W. W. Greg, *The Editorial Problem in Shakespeare*; R. B. McKerrow, *Prolegomena for the Oxford Shakespeare*; Charlton Hinman's Introduction to *The Norton Facsimile* of the First Folio; and for particular plays to Dover Wilson's 'Notes on the Copy' in the New Cambridge Shakespeare.

Page 94

18 Granville-Barker's detailed exposition of 'The Three Days' Battle' is to be found in his preface to ANTONY AND CLEOPATRA (Second Series, 143 ff.).

19 Percy Simpson, *Shakespearian Punctuation* (1911); Chambers, I.190 ff.; Ridley's Arden edition of ANTONY AND CLEOPATRA (xi ff.) and of OTHELLO (209 ff.); R. Flatter, *Shakespeare's Producing Hand*, 136 ff. Flatter's whole chapter should be read, and indeed his whole book, of which Nevill Coghill, in a foreword, gives his opinion that 'no producer, actor or editor who himself aims at distinction in Shakespearian work can afford to ignore Dr. Flatter's revolutionary discoveries'.

Page 97

20 It is said that the speech of Shakespeare's England can still be heard in certain parts of the New World—such as Barbados and the Appalachian Mountains—where the language has suffered no refinement of later invasion. The exact sound of Shakespeare's words, as spoken by his fellow-actors, has been the subject of much interesting research, and also of practical experiment in performance. Distant recollection of one such occasion records that the performance succeeded very well with an audience composed largely of the 'judicious'. It was a treat for the connoisseurs, who quickly accepted the unfamiliar music of Elizabethan vowel-sounds, but would, no doubt, have been caviare to the general. Moreover, the speech of the actors, dedicated to their task of scholarly rehabilitation, neutralised the variety of diction. So when we want to know how Shakespeare's text sounded in his own playhouse, we make a reservation for the convenience of our readers: just as we have thought fit to translate the spelling of the Quartos and Folio, so too we take leave to listen with modern ears: the sound and the shape of Shakespeare's dramatic poetry is little impaired by this translation, and the sense is much more easily communicated by the player and understood by the audience.

Page 99
21 In the Folio text of HAMLET, I.v, *lines* 56–57 are printed as a single line, thus:

Will sate it selfe in a Celestiall bed, & prey on Garbage.

Charlton Hinman (*The Norton Facsimile*, xvii) has shown that this mislineation occurs at the bottom of an unusually crowded page and the compositor has taken a pardonably sensible way out of his problem: 'by representing the word "and" with an ampersand, it has been possible to squeeze two verse-lines into one line of type. Though the second of these verse-lines is abnormally short, it should occupy a separate line of type—as it does in the good quarto version of the play.'

Page 102
22 Flatter (73 ff.) has a chapter on line-division, with many interesting examples of the misleading 'regularization' of editors. He does not, however, reach the logical conclusion that the most satisfactory method for a modern editor is to print each speech close to its speech-heading.

Page 104
23 Ridley's discussion of 'The Textual Problem' in the Arden edition of OTHELLO is helpful not only in its consideration of particularities but also in its illumination of the general issues of textual comparison.

Page 106
24 Muir's second volume, in which discussion of the Histories is promised, is still awaited with impatient interest. A detailed exploration of Shakespeare's creative process is to be found in David P. Young's *Something of Great Constancy*, in which the 'Backgrounds', both dramatic and non-dramatic, of A MID-SUMMER NIGHT'S DREAM are analysed in depth.

Page 140
25 Flatter, 37 f.

Page 151
26 An admirable chapter on this theme appears in Coghill's *Shakespeare's Professional Skills*.

SELECT BIBLIOGRAPHY

ADAMS, JOHN CRANFORD, *The Globe Playhouse* (Cambridge, Mass., 1943)

BALDWIN, T. W., *The Organization and Personnel of the Shakespearean Company* (Princeton, 1927)

BECKERMAN, BERNARD, *Shakespeare at the Globe 1599–1609* (New York, 1962)

BENTLEY, GERALD EADES, *Shakespeare and His Theater* (Lincoln, Nebraska, 1964)

BRADBROOK, M. C., *Elizabethan Stage Conditions* (Cambridge, 1968)

——, *Shakespeare the Craftsman* (1969)

——, *The Rise of the Common Player* (1962)

BULLOUGH, GEOFFREY, *Narrative and Dramatic Sources of Shakespeare*, 7 vols (1957–70)

CHAMBERS, E. K., *William Shakespeare*, 2 vols (Oxford, 1930)

CLEMEN, W. H., *The Development of Shakespeare's Imagery* (1951)

COGHILL, NEVILL, *Shakespeare's Professional Skills* (Cambridge, 1964)

CUTTS, JOHN P., *Musique de la Troupe de Shakespeare* (Paris, 1959)

DE BANKE, CÉCILE, *Shakespearean Stage Production* (1954)

FLATTER, RICHARD, *Shakespeare's Producing Hand* (1948)

GRANVILLE-BARKER, HARLEY, *Prefaces to Shakespeare* (1927, 1930)

GREG, W. W., *The Editorial Problem in Shakespeare* (Oxford, 1942)

——, *Dramatic Documents from the Elizabethan Playhouses*, 2 vols (Oxford, 1931)

GURR, ANDREW, *The Shakespearean Stage 1574–1642* (Cambridge, 1970)

HARBAGE, ALFRED, *Shakespeare's Audience* (New York, 1941)

——, *Conceptions of Shakespeare* (Cambridge, Mass., 1966)

HINMAN, CHARLTON, *The First Folio of Shakespeare, The Norton Facsimile* (New York, 1968)

Hodges, C. Walter, *The Globe Restored* (1968)

——, *Shakespeare's Theatre* (1964)

Holmes, Martin, *Shakespeare and His Players* (1972)

Hotson, Leslie, *Shakespeare's Motley* (1952)

Joseph, B. L., *Elizabethan Acting* (Oxford, 1964)

King, T. J., *Shakespearean Staging 1599–1642* (Cambridge, Mass., 1971)

Linthicum, M. Channing, *Costume in Elizabethan Drama* (Oxford, 1936)

McKerrow, Ronald B., *Prolegomena for the Oxford Shakespeare* (Oxford, 1939)

Muir, Kenneth, *Shakespeare's Sources*, vol. 1 (1957)

——, and Schoenbaum, S., *A New Companion to Shakespeare Studies* (Cambridge, 1971)

Nagler, A. M., *Shakespeare's Stage* (New Haven, Conn., 1958)

Naylor, Edward W., *Shakespeare and Music* (1931)

——, *Shakespeare Music* (1928)

Noble, Richmond, *Shakespeare's Use of Song* (Oxford, 1923)

Reese, M. M., *Shakespeare, His World and His Work* (1953)

Reynolds, George F., *On Shakespeare's Stage* (ed. Knaub, Boulder, Col., 1967)

Shirley, Frances A., *Shakespeare's Use of Off-Stage Sounds* (Lincoln, Nebraska, 1963)

Simpson, Percy, *Shakespearian Punctuation* (Oxford, 1911)

Smith, Irwin, *Shakespeare's Blackfriars Playhouse* (New York, 1964)

Spurgeon, Caroline F. E., *Shakespeare's Imagery* (Cambridge, 1935)

Styan, J. L., *Shakespeare's Stagecraft* (Cambridge, 1967)

Watkins, Ronald, *On Producing Shakespeare* (1950)

Wickham, Glynne H., *Early English Stages*, vol. 2 (1963, 1972)

Yates, Frances A., *Theatre of the World* (1969)

Young, David P., *Something of Great Constancy* (New Haven, Conn., 1966)

INDEX